Learning QGIS

Third Edition

The latest guide to using QGIS 2.14 to create great maps and perform geoprocessing tasks with ease

Anita Graser

community experience distilled

BIRMINGHAM - MUMBAI

Learning QGIS
Third Edition

First published: September 2013

Second edition: December 2014

Third edition: March 2016

Production reference: 1030316

Published by Packt Publishing Ltd.
Livery Place
35 Livery Street
Birmingham B3 2PB, UK.

ISBN 978-1-78588-033-9

www.packtpub.com

Credits

Author
Anita Graser

Reviewer
Cornelius Roth

Commissioning Editor
Veena Pagare

Acquisition Editor
Larissa Pinto

Content Development Editor
Prashanth G. Rao

Technical Editor
Tanmayee Patil

Copy Editor
Vikrant Phadke

Project Coordinator
Bijal Patel

Proofreader
Safis Editing

Indexer
Mariammal Chettiyar

Production Coordinator
Arvindkumar Gupta

Cover Work
Arvindkumar Gupta

About the Author

Anita Graser studied geomatics at the University of Applied Sciences Wiener Neustadt, Austria, from where she graduated with a master's degree in 2010. During her studies, she gained hands-on experience in the fields of geo-marketing and transportation research. Since 2007, she has been working as a geographic information systems (GIS) expert with the dynamic transportation systems group at the Austrian Institute of Technology (AIT), where she focuses on analyzing and visualizing spatio-temporal data. Anita serves on the OSGeo board of directors and the QGIS project steering committee. She has been working with GIS since 2005, provides QGIS training courses, and writes a popular blog on open source GIS at `anitagraser.com`.

I would like to say thanks to my family, partner, and coworkers for their support and encouragement. Of course, I also want to thank the whole QGIS community for their continued efforts to provide the best open source GIS experience possible and everyone who made the previous editions of *Learning QGIS* such great successes.

About the Reviewer

Cornelius Roth holds a master's degree in geography and geoinformatics at the University of Salzburg. He is currently working at the Department of Geoinformatics on research projects, helping them use GIS-related methods in emergency and air traffic management, open source GIS, and open data.

Recently, he has also worked at the economic development agency BGL, Bavaria, with a strong focus on fostering companies when applying GIS methods and services to support their business objectives. As a third pillar, Cornelius manages e-learning courses for the UNIGIS distance learning network in Salzburg.

www.PacktPub.com

eBooks, discount offers, and more

Did you know that Packt offers eBook versions of every book published, with PDF and ePub files available? You can upgrade to the eBook version at www.PacktPub.com and as a print book customer, you are entitled to a discount on the eBook copy. Get in touch with us at customercare@packtpub.com for more details.

At www.PacktPub.com, you can also read a collection of free technical articles, sign up for a range of free newsletters and receive exclusive discounts and offers on Packt books and eBooks.

https://www2.packtpub.com/books/subscription/packtlib

Do you need instant solutions to your IT questions? PacktLib is Packt's online digital book library. Here, you can search, access, and read Packt's entire library of books.

Why subscribe?

- Fully searchable across every book published by Packt
- Copy and paste, print, and bookmark content
- On demand and accessible via a web browser

Table of Contents

Preface

Welcome to the third edition of *Learning QGIS*. This book aims to introduce you to QGIS 2.14 and show you how to perform core geospatial tasks using this popular open source GIS. It takes you through six chapters from QGIS installation and setup in the first chapter, to the essentials of viewing spatial data in the second chapter. The third chapter covers data creation and editing, followed by the fourth chapter, which offers an introduction to performing spatial analysis in QGIS. In the fifth chapter, you will learn how to create great maps and how to prepare them for print, and the final chapter shows you how you can extend QGIS using the Python scripting language.

What this book covers

Chapter 1, Getting Started with QGIS, covers the installation and configuration of QGIS. We will also see the user interface and how to customize it. By the end of this chapter, you will have QGIS running on your machine and be ready to start with the tutorials.

Chapter 2, Viewing Spatial Data, covers how to view spatial data from different data sources. QGIS supports many file and database formats as well as OGC web services. We will first see how we can load layers from these different data sources. Then, we will look into the basics of styling both vector and raster layers and will create our first map. We will finish this chapter with an example for loading background maps from online services.

Chapter 3, Data Creation and Editing, covers how to create and manipulate spatial datasets. We will cover how to select features and take measurements before we continue with editing feature geometries and attributes. We will then reproject vector and raster data and learn how to convert between different file formats. Furthermore, we will join data from text files and spreadsheets to our spatial data. We will also explore the use of temporary scratch layers, learn how to fix common topological errors, and finally, how to load data into spatial databases.

Chapter 4, Spatial Analysis, covers raster processing and analyses tasks such as clipping and terrain analysis. Then we cover converting between raster and vector formats before we continue with common vector geoprocessing tasks such as generating heatmaps and calculating area shares within a region. Finally, we will finish the chapter with exercises in automating geoprocessing workflows using the QGIS Processing modeler and leveraging the power of spatial databases for analysis.

Chapter 5, Creating Great Maps, covers important features that enable us to create great maps. We will go into advanced vector styling, building on what we learned in *Chapter 2, Viewing Spatial Data*. Then, we will cover labeling using examples of labeling point locations as well as creating more advanced road labels with road shield graphics. We will also cover how to tweak labels manually. We will get to know the print composer and how to use it to create printable maps and map books. Finally, we will cover solutions to present your maps on the Web.

Chapter 6, Extending QGIS with Python, covers scripting QGIS with Python. We will start with an introduction to actions before we get started with the QGIS Python Console and more advanced development of custom tools for the Processing toolbox. Finally, we will cover how to create our own plugins.

What you need for this book

To follow the exercises in this book, you need QGIS 2.14. QGIS installation is covered in the first chapter and download links for the exercise data are provided in the respective chapters.

Who this book is for

If you are a user, developer, or consultant and want to know how to use QGIS to achieve the results you are used to from other GIS, this is the book for you. This book is not intended to be a GIS textbook. You, the reader, are expected to be comfortable with core GIS concepts.

Conventions

In this book, you will find a number of text styles that distinguish between different kinds of information. Here are some examples of these styles and an explanation of their meaning.

Code words in text, database table names, folder names, filenames, file extensions, pathnames, dummy URLs, user input, and Twitter handles are shown as follows: "use `[% $now %]` to insert the current time stamp".

A block of code is set as follows:

```
( landcover@1 > 0 AND landcover@1 <= 6 ) * 100
+ ( landcover@1 >= 7 AND landcover@1 <= 10 ) * 101
+ ( landcover@1 >= 11 ) * 102
```

When we wish to draw your attention to a particular part of a code block, the relevant lines or items are set in bold:

```
def initGui(self):
    # create the toolbar icon and menu entry
    icon_path = ':/plugins/MyFirstMapTool/icon.png'
    self.map_tool_action=self.add_action(
        icon_path,
        text=self.tr(u'My 1st Map Tool'),
        callback=self.map_tool_init,
        parent=self.iface.mainWindow())
    self.map_tool_action.setCheckable(True)
```

Any command-line input or output is written as follows:

```
sudo apt-get install qgis python-qgis qgis-plugin-grass
```

New terms and **important words** are shown in bold. Words that you see on the screen, for example, in menus or dialog boxes, appear in the text like this: "To add text to the map, we can use the **Add new label** button or go to **Layout | Add label**".

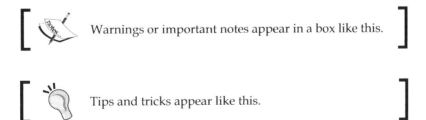

Warnings or important notes appear in a box like this.

Tips and tricks appear like this.

Reader feedback

Feedback from our readers is always welcome. Let us know what you think about this book—what you liked or disliked. Reader feedback is important for us as it helps us develop titles that you will really get the most out of.

To send us general feedback, simply e-mail feedback@packtpub.com, and mention the book's title in the subject of your message.

If there is a topic that you have expertise in and you are interested in either writing or contributing to a book, see our author guide at www.packtpub.com/authors.

Customer support

Now that you are the proud owner of a Packt book, we have a number of things to help you to get the most from your purchase.

Downloading the example code

You can download the example code files for this book from your account at http://www.packtpub.com. If you purchased this book elsewhere, you can visit http://www.packtpub.com/support and register to have the files e-mailed directly to you.

You can download the code files by following these steps:

1. Log in or register to our website using your e-mail address and password.
2. Hover the mouse pointer on the **SUPPORT** tab at the top.
3. Click on **Code Downloads & Errata**.
4. Enter the name of the book in the **Search** box.
5. Select the book for which you're looking to download the code files.
6. Choose from the drop-down menu where you purchased this book from.
7. Click on **Code Download**.

Once the file is downloaded, please make sure that you unzip or extract the folder using the latest version of:

- WinRAR / 7-Zip for Windows
- Zipeg / iZip / UnRarX for Mac
- 7-Zip / PeaZip for Linux

Downloading the color images of this book

We also provide you with a PDF file that has color images of the screenshots/ diagrams used in this book. The color images will help you better understand the changes in the output. You can download this file from `https://www.packtpub. com/sites/default/files/downloads/Learning_QGIS_Third_Edition_ ColorImages.pdf`.

Errata

Although we have taken every care to ensure the accuracy of our content, mistakes do happen. If you find a mistake in one of our books—maybe a mistake in the text or the code—we would be grateful if you could report this to us. By doing so, you can save other readers from frustration and help us improve subsequent versions of this book. If you find any errata, please report them by visiting `http://www.packtpub. com/submit-errata`, selecting your book, clicking on the **Errata Submission Form** link, and entering the details of your errata. Once your errata are verified, your submission will be accepted and the errata will be uploaded to our website or added to any list of existing errata under the Errata section of that title.

To view the previously submitted errata, go to `https://www.packtpub.com/books/ content/support` and enter the name of the book in the search field. The required information will appear under the **Errata** section.

Piracy

Piracy of copyrighted material on the Internet is an ongoing problem across all media. At Packt, we take the protection of our copyright and licenses very seriously. If you come across any illegal copies of our works in any form on the Internet, please provide us with the location address or website name immediately so that we can pursue a remedy.

Please contact us at `copyright@packtpub.com` with a link to the suspected pirated material.

We appreciate your help in protecting our authors and our ability to bring you valuable content.

Questions

If you have a problem with any aspect of this book, you can contact us at `questions@packtpub.com`, and we will do our best to address the problem.

1
Getting Started with QGIS

In this chapter, we will install and configure the **QGIS** geographic information system. We will also get to know the user interface and how to customize it. By the end of this chapter, you will have QGIS running on your machine and be ready to start with the tutorials.

Installing QGIS

QGIS runs on **Windows**, various **Linux** distributions, **Unix**, **Mac OS X**, and **Android**. The QGIS project provides ready-to-use packages as well as instructions to build from the source code at http://download.qgis.org. We will cover how to install QGIS on two systems, Windows and Ubuntu, as well as how to avoid the most common pitfalls.

> Further installation instructions for other supported operating systems are available at http://www.qgis.org/en/site/forusers/alldownloads.html.

Like many other open source projects, QGIS offers you a choice between different releases. For the tutorials in this book, we will use the **QGIS 2.14 LTR** version. The following options are available:

- **Long-term release (LTR)**: The LTR version is recommended for corporate and academic use. It is currently released once per year in the end of February. It receives bug fix updates for at least a year, and the features and user interface remain unchanged. This makes it the best choice for training material that should not become outdated after a few months.

- **Latest release (LR)**: The LR version contains newly developed and tested features. It is currently released every four months (except when an LTR version is released instead). Use this version if you want to stay up to date with the latest developments, including new features and user interface changes, but are not comfortable with using the DEV version.

- **Developer version (DEV, master, or testing)**: The cutting-edge DEV version contains the latest and greatest developments, but be warned that on some days, it might not work as reliably as you want it to.

> You can find more information about the releases as well as the schedule for future releases at `http://www.qgis.org/en/site/getinvolved/development/roadmap.html#release-schedule`.
>
> For an overview of the changes between releases, check out the visual change logs at `http://www.qgis.org/en/site/forusers/visualchangelogs.html`.

Installing QGIS on Windows

On Windows, we have two different options to install QGIS, the standalone installer and the **OSGeo4W** installer:

- The **standalone installer** is one big file to download (approximately 280 MB); it contains a QGIS release, the **Geographic Resources Analysis Support System (GRASS)** GIS, as well as the **System for Automated Geoscientific Analyses (SAGA)** GIS in one package.

- The **OSGeo4W installer** is a small, flexible installation tool that makes it possible to download and install QGIS and many more OSGeo tools with all their dependencies. The main advantage of this installer over the standalone installer is that it makes updating QGIS and its dependencies very easy. You can always have access to both the current release and the developer versions if you choose to, but, of course, you are never forced to update. That is why I recommend that you use **OSGeo4W**. You can download the 32-bit and 64-bit OSGeo4W installers from `http://osgeo4w.osgeo.org` (or directly from `http://download.osgeo.org/osgeo4w/osgeo4w-setup-x86.exe` for the 32-bit version or `http://download.osgeo.org/osgeo4w-setup-x86_64.exe` if you have a 64-bit version of Windows). Download the version that matches your operating system and keep it! In the future, whenever you want to change or update your system, just run it again.

Regardless of the installer you choose, make sure that you avoid special characters such as German umlauts or letters from alphabets other than the default Latin ones (for details, refer to https://en.wikipedia.org/wiki/ISO_basic_Latin_alphabet) in the installation path, as they can cause problems later on, for example, during plugin installation.

When the OSGeo4W installer starts, we get to choose between **Express Desktop Install**, **Express Web-GIS Install**, and **Advanced Install**. To install the QGIS LR version, we can simply select the **Express Desktop Install** option, and the next dialog will list the available desktop applications, such as **QGIS**, **uDig**, and **GRASS GIS**. We can simply select **QGIS**, click on **Next**, and confirm the necessary dependencies by clicking on **Next** again. Then the download and installation will start automatically. When the installation is complete, there will be desktop shortcuts and start menu entries for OSGeo4W and QGIS.

To install QGIS LTR (or DEV), we need to go through the **Advanced Install** option, as shown in the following screenshot:

This installation path offers many options, such as **Download Without Installing** and **Install from Local Directory**, which can be used to download all the necessary packages on one machine and later install them on machines without Internet access. We just select **Install from Internet**, as shown in this screenshot:

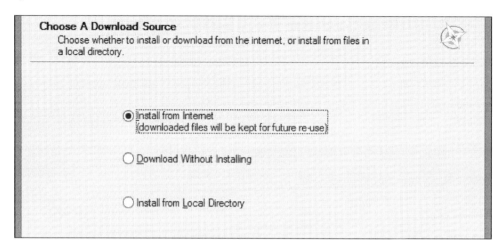

When selecting the installation **Root Directory**, as shown in the following screenshot, avoid special characters such as German umlauts or letters from alphabets other than the default Latin ones in the installation path (as mentioned before), as they can cause problems later on, for example, during plugin installation:

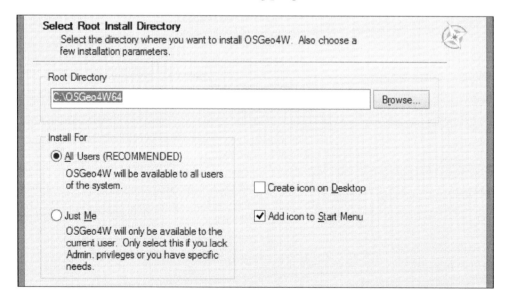

Then you can specify the folder (**Local Package Directory**) where the setup process will store the installation files as well as customize **Start menu name**. I recommend that you leave the default settings similar to what you can see in this screenshot:

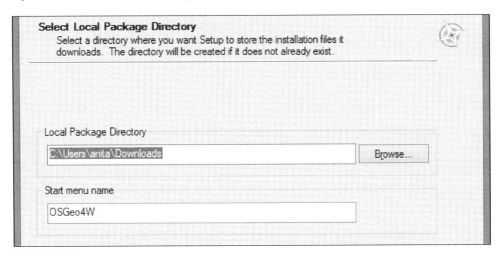

In the Internet connection settings, it is usually not necessary to change the default settings, but if your machine is, for example, hidden behind a **proxy**, you will be able to specify it here:

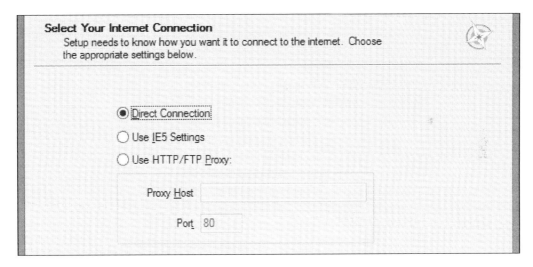

Then we can pick the *download site*. At the time of writing this book, there is only one download server available, anyway, as you can see in the following screenshot:

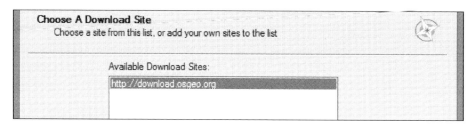

After the installer fetches the latest package information from OSGeo's servers, we get to pick the packages for installation. QGIS LTR is listed in the desktop category as **qgis-ltr** (and the DEV version is listed as **qgis-dev**). To select the LTR version for installation, click on the text that reads **Skip**, and it will change and display the version number, as shown in this screenshot:

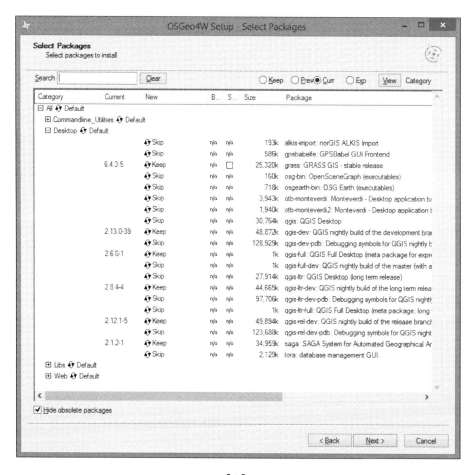

As you can see in the following screenshot, the installer will automatically select all the necessary dependencies (such as GDAL, SAGA, OTB, and GRASS), so we don't have to worry about this:

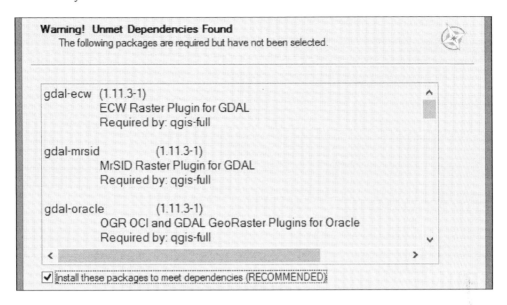

After you've clicked on **Next**, the download and installation starts automatically, just as in the Express version.

You have probably noticed other available QGIS packages called **qgis-ltr-dev** and **qgis-rel-dev**. These contain the latest changes (to the LTR and LR versions, respectively), which will be released as bug fix versions according to the release schedule. This makes these packages a good option if you run into an issue with a release that has been fixed recently but the bug fix version release is not out yet.

If you try to run QGIS and get a popup that says, **The procedure entry point <some-name> could not be located in the dynamic link library <dll-name>.dll**, it means that you are facing a common issue on Windows systems—a *DLL conflict*. This error is easy to fix; just copy the DLL file mentioned in the error message from `C:\OSGeo4W\bin\` to `C:\OSGeo4W\apps\qgis\bin\` (adjust the paths if necessary).

Installing on Ubuntu

On Ubuntu, the QGIS project provides packages for the LTR, LR, and DEV versions. At the time of writing this book, the Ubuntu versions Precise, Trusty, Vivid, and Wily are supported, but you can find the latest information at `http://www.qgis.org/en/site/forusers/alldownloads.html#debian-ubuntu`. Be aware, however, that you can install only one version at a time. The packages are not listed in the default Ubuntu repositories. Therefore, we have to add the appropriate repositories to Ubuntu's source list, which you can find at `/etc/apt/sources.list`. You can open the file with any text editor. Make sure that you have super user rights, as you will need them to save your edits. One option is to use `gedit`, which is installed in Ubuntu by default. To edit the `sources.list` file, use the following command:

```
sudo gedit /etc/apt/sources.list
```

Downloading the example code

You can download the example code files for this book from your account at `http://www.packtpub.com`. If you purchased this book elsewhere, you can visit `http://www.packtpub.com/support` and register to have the files e-mailed directly to you.

Make sure that you add only one of the following package-source options to avoid conflicts due to incompatible packages. The specific lines that you have to add to the source list depend on your Ubuntu version:

1. *The first option*, which is also the default one, is to install the LR version. To install the QGIS LR release on Trusty, add the following lines to your file:

   ```
   deb      http://qgis.org/debian trusty main
   deb-src http://qgis.org/debian trusty main
   ```

   If necessary, replace `trusty` with `precise`, `vivid`, or `wily` to fit your system. For an updated list of supported Ubuntu versions, check out `http://www.qgis.org/en/site/forusers/alldownloads.html#debian-ubuntu`.

2. *The second option* is to install QGIS LTR by adding the following lines to your file:

   ```
   deb      http://qgis.org/debian-ltr trusty main
   deb-src http://qgis.org/debian-ltr trusty main
   ```

3. *The third option* is to install QGIS DEV by adding these lines to your file:

```
deb      http://qgis.org/debian-nightly trusty main
deb-src http://qgis.org/debian-nightly trusty main
```

 The preceding versions depend on other packages such as GDAL and proj4, which are available in the Ubuntu repositories. It is worth mentioning that these packages are often quite old.

4. *The fourth option* is to install QGIS LR with updated dependencies, which are provided by the ubuntugis repository. Add these lines to your file:

```
deb      http://qgis.org/ubuntugis trusty main
deb-src http://qgis.org/ubuntugis trusty main
deb      http://ppa.launchpad.net/ubuntugis/ubuntugis-unstable/
ubuntu trusty main
```

5. *The fifth option* is QGIS LTR with updated dependencies. Add these lines to your file:

```
deb      http://qgis.org/ubuntugis-ltr trusty main
deb-src http://qgis.org/ubuntugis-ltr trusty main
deb      http://ppa.launchpad.net/ubuntugis/ubuntugis-unstable/
ubuntu trusty main
```

6. *The sixth option* is the QGIS master with updated dependencies. Add these lines to your file:

```
deb      http://qgis.org/ubuntugis-nightly trusty main
deb-src http://qgis.org/ubuntugis-nightly trusty main
deb      http://ppa.launchpad.net/ubuntugis/ubuntugis-unstable/
ubuntu trusty main
```

 To follow the tutorials in this book, it is recommended that you install QGIS 2.14 LTR with updated dependencies (the fifth option).

After choosing the repository, we will add the qgis.org repository's public key to our apt keyring. This will avoid the warnings that you might otherwise get when installing from a non-default repository. Run the following command in the terminal:

```
sudo apt-key adv --keyserver keyserver.ubuntu.com --recv-key
3FF5FFCAD71472C4
```

By the time this book goes to print, the key information might have changed. Refer to `http://www.qgis.org/en/site/forusers/alldownloads.html#debian-ubuntu` for the latest updates.

Finally, to install QGIS, run the following commands:

```
sudo apt-get update
sudo apt-get install qgis python-qgis qgis-plugin-grass
```

Running QGIS for the first time

When you install QGIS, you will get two applications: **QGIS Desktop** and **QGIS Browser**. If you are familiar with **ArcGIS**, you can think of QGIS Browser as something similar to **ArcCatalog**. It is a small application used to preview spatial data and related metadata. For the remainder of this book, we will focus on QGIS Desktop.

By default, QGIS will use the operating system's default language. To follow the tutorials in this book, I advise you to change the language to English by going to **Settings** | **Options** | **Locale**.

On the first run, the way the toolbars are arranged can hide some buttons. To be able to work efficiently, I suggest that you rearrange the toolbars (for the sake of completeness, I have enabled all toolbars in **Toolbars**, which is in the **View** menu). I like to place some toolbars on the left and right screen borders to save vertical screen estate, especially on wide-screen displays.

Additionally, we will activate the file browser by navigating to **View** | **Panels** | **Browser Panel**. It will provide us with quick access to our spatial data. At the end, the QGIS window on your screen should look similar to the following screenshot:

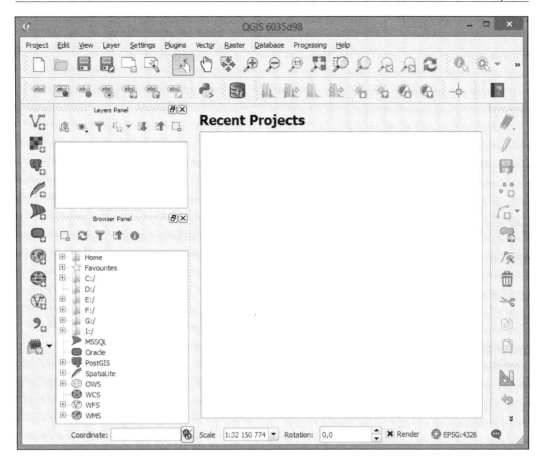

Next, we will activate some must-have plugins by navigating to **Plugins | Manage and Install Plugins**. Plugins are activated by ticking the checkboxes beside their names. To begin with, I will recommend the following:

- **Coordinate Capture**: This plugin is useful for picking coordinates in the map
- **DB Manager**: This plugin helps you manage the SpatiaLite and PostGIS databases
- **fTools**: This plugin offers vector analysis and management tools
- **GdalTools**: This plugin offers raster analysis and management tools
- **Processing**: This plugin provides access to many useful raster and vector analysis tools, as well as a model builder for task automation

To make it easier to find specific plugins, we can filter the list of plugins using the **Search** input field at the top of the window, which you can see in the following screenshot:

Introducing the QGIS user interface

Now that we have set up QGIS, let's get accustomed to the interface. As we have already seen in the screenshot presented in the *Running QGIS for the first time* section, the biggest area is reserved for the map. To the left of the map, there are the **Layers** and **Browser** panels. In the following screenshot, you can see how the **Layers Panel** looks once we have loaded some layers (which we will do in the upcoming *Chapter 2, Viewing Spatial Data*). To the left of each layer entry, you can see a preview of the layer style. Additionally, we can use **layer group** to structure the layer list. The **Browser Panel** (on the right-hand side in the following screenshot) provides us with quick access to our spatial data, as you will soon see in the following chapter:

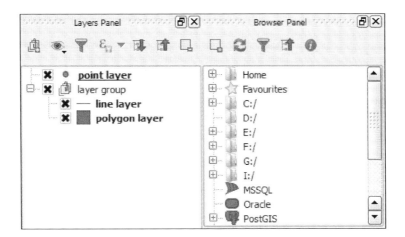

Below the map, we find important information such as (from left to right)
the current map **Coordinate**, map **Scale**, and the (currently inactive) project
coordinate reference system (**CRS**), for example, **EPSG:4326** in this screenshot:

Next, there are multiple toolbars to explore. If you arrange them as shown in the
previous section, the top row contains the following toolbars:

- **File**: This toolbar contains the tools needed to **Create**, **Open**, **Save**,
  and **Print projects**

- **Map Navigation**: This toolbar contains the pan and zoom tools

- **Attributes**: These tools are used to *identify*, *select*, *open attribute tables*, *measure*,
  and so on, and looks like this:

The second row contains the following toolbars:

- **Label**: These tools are used to add, configure, and modify labels

- **Plugins**: This currently only contains the **Python Console** tool, but will be
  filled in by additional Python plugins

- **Database**: Currently, this toolbar only contains DB Manager, but other
  database-related tools (for example, the **OfflineEditing** plugin, which allows
  us to edit offline and synchronize with databases) will appear here when
  they are installed

- **Raster**: This toolbar includes histogram stretch, brightness, and contrast control

- **Vector**: This currently only contains the **Coordinate Capture** tool, but it will be filled in by additional Python plugins

- **Web**: This is currently empty, but it will also be filled in by additional Python plugins

- **Help**: This toolbar points to the option for downloading the user manual and looks like this:

On the left screen border, we place the **Manage Layers** toolbar. This toolbar contains the tools for adding layers from the *vector or raster files*, *databases*, *web services*, and *text files* or *create new layers*:

Finally, on the right screen border, we have two more toolbars:

- **Digitizing**: The tools in this toolbar **enable editing**, basic feature creation, and editing

- **Advanced Digitizing**: This toolbar contains the **Undo/Redo** option, **advanced editing tools**, **the geometry-simplification tool**, and so on, which look like this:

 All digitizing tools (except the **Enable advanced digitizing tools** button) are currently inactive. They will turn active only once we start editing a vector layer.

Toolbars and panels can be activated and deactivated via the **View** menu's **Panels** and **Toolbars** entries, as well as by right-clicking on a menu or toolbar, which will open a context menu with all the available toolbars and panels. All the tools on the toolbars can also be accessed via the menu. If you deactivate the **Manage Layers Toolbar**, for example, you will still be able to add layers using the **Layer** menu.

As you might have guessed by now, QGIS is highly customizable. You can increase your productivity by assigning shortcuts to the tools you use regularly, which you can do by going to **Settings | Configure Shortcuts**. Similarly, if you realize that you never use a certain toolbar button or menu entry, you can hide it by going to **Settings | Customization**. For example, if you don't have access to an Oracle Spatial database, you might want to hide the associated buttons to remove clutter and save screen estate, as shown in the following screenshot:

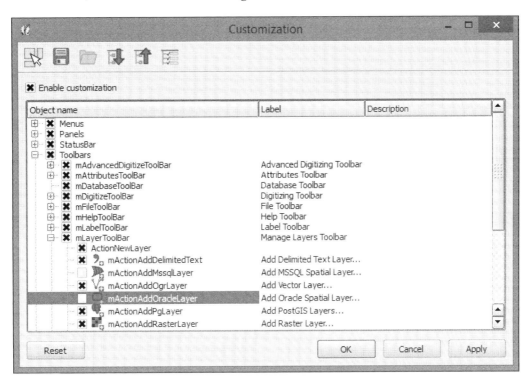

Finding help and reporting issues

The QGIS community offers a variety of different community-based support options. These include the following:

- **GIS StackExchange**: One of the most popular support channels is `http://gis.stackexchange.com/`. It's a general-purpose GIS question-and-answer site. If you use the tag `qgis`, you will see all QGIS-related questions and answers at `http://gis.stackexchange.com/questions/tagged/qgis`.

- **Mailing lists**: The most important mailing list for user questions is `qgis-user`. For a full list of available mailing lists and links to sign up, visit `http://www.qgis.org/en/site/getinvolved/mailinglists.html#qgis-mailinglists`. To comfortably search for existing mailing list threads, you can use Nabble (`http://osgeo-org.1560.x6.nabble.com/Quantum-GIS-User-f4125267.html`).

- **Chat**: A lot of developer communication runs through IRC. There is a `#qgis` channel on `www.freenode.net`. You can visit it using, for example, the web interface at `http://webchat.freenode.net/?channels=#qgis`.

 Before contacting the community support, it's recommended to first take a look at the documentation at `http://docs.qgis.org`.

If you prefer commercial support, you can find a list of companies that provide support and custom development at `http://www.qgis.org/en/site/forusers/commercial_support.html#qgis-commercial-support`.

If you find a bug, please report it because the QGIS developers can only fix the bugs that they are aware of. For details on how to report bugs, visit `http://www.qgis.org/en/site/getinvolved/development/bugreporting.html`.

Summary

In this chapter, we installed QGIS and configured it by selecting useful defaults and arranging the user interface elements. Then we explored the panels, toolbars, and menus that make up the QGIS user interface, and you learned how to customize them to increase productivity. In the following chapter, we will use QGIS to view spatial data from different data sources such as files, databases, and web services in order to create our first map.

2
Viewing Spatial Data

In this chapter, we will cover how to view spatial data from different data sources. QGIS supports many file and database formats as well as standardized **Open Geospatial Consortium** (**OGC**) Web Services. We will first cover how we can load layers from these different data sources. We will then look into the basics of styling both vector and raster layers and will create our first map, which you can see in the following screenshot:

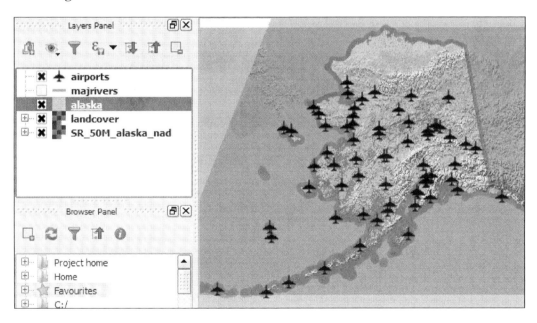

We will finish this chapter with an example of loading background maps from online services.

For the examples in this chapter, we will use the sample data
provided by the QGIS project, which is available for download
from `http://qgis.org/downloads/data/qgis_sample_`
`data.zip` (21 MB). Download and unzip it.

Loading vector data from files

In this section, we will talk about loading vector data from GIS file formats, such as
shapefiles, as well as from text files.

We can load vector files by going to **Layer** | **Add Layer** | **Add Vector Layer** and also
using the **Add Vector Layer** toolbar button. If you like shortcuts, use *Ctrl + Shift + V*.
In the **Add vector layer** dialog, which is shown in the following screenshot, we find a
drop-down list that allows us to specify the encoding of the input file. This option is
important if we are dealing with files that contain special characters, such as German
umlauts or letters from alphabets different from the default Latin ones.

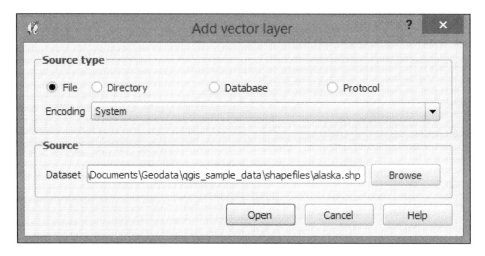

What we are most interested in now is the **Browse** button, which opens the
file-opening dialog. Note the file type filter drop-down list in the bottom-right corner
of the dialog. We can open it to see a list of supported vector file types. This filter
is useful to find specific files faster by hiding all the files of a different type, but be
aware that the filter settings are stored and will be applied again the next time you
open the file opening dialog. This can be a source of confusion if you try to find a
different file later and it happens to be hidden by the filter, so remember to check the
filter settings if you are having trouble locating a file.

We can load more than one file in one go by selecting multiple files at once (holding down *Ctrl* on Windows/Ubuntu or *cmd* on Mac). Let's give it a try:

1. First, we select `alaska.shp` and `airports.shp` from the `shapefiles` sample data folder.

2. Next, we confirm our selection by clicking on **Open**, and we are taken back to the **Add vector layer** dialog.

3. After we've clicked on **Open** once more, the selected files are loaded. You will notice that each vector layer is displayed in a random color, which is most likely different from the color that you see in the following screenshot. Don't worry about this now; we'll deal with layer styles later in this chapter.

Even without us using any spatial analysis tools, these simple steps of visualizing spatial datasets enable us to find, for example, the southernmost airport on the Alaskan mainland.

There are multiple tricks that make loading data even faster; for example, you can simply drag and drop files from the operating system's file browser into QGIS.

Another way to quickly access your spatial data is by using QGIS's built-in file *browser*. If you have set up QGIS as shown in *Chapter 1*, *Getting Started with QGIS*, you'll find the browser on the left-hand side, just below the layer list. Navigate to your `data` folder, and you can again drag and drop files from the browser to the map.

Additionally, you can mark a folder as *favorite* by right-clicking on it and selecting **Add as a favorite**. In this way, you can access your data folders even faster, because they are added in the **Favorites** section right at the top of the browser list.

Another popular source of spatial data is **delimited text (CSV)** files. QGIS can load CSV files using the **Add Delimited Text Layer** option available via the menu entry by going to **Layer | Add Layer | Add Delimited Text Layer** or the corresponding toolbar button. Click on **Browse** and select `elevp.csv` from the sample data. CSV files come with all kinds of delimiters. As you can see in the following screenshot, the plugin lets you choose from the most common ones (**Comma, Tab**, and so on), but you can also specify any other plain or regular-expression delimiter:

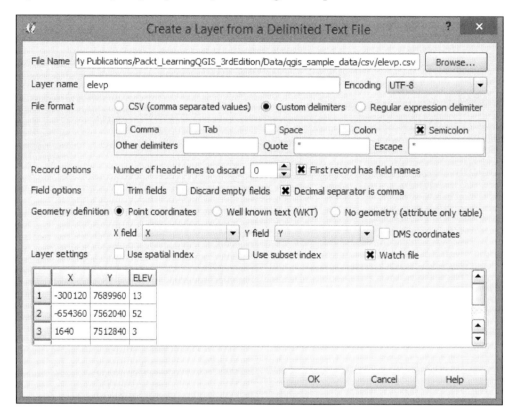

If your CSV file contains quotation marks such as, " or ', you can use the **Quote** option to have them removed. The **Number of header lines to discard** option allows us to skip any potential extra lines at the beginning of the text file. The following **Field options** include functionality for trimming extra spaces from field values or redefine the decimal separator to a comma. The spatial information itself can be provided either in the two columns that contain the coordinates of points *X* and *Y*, or using the **Well known text (WKT)** format. A WKT field can contain points, lines, or polygons. For example, a point can be specified as `POINT (30 10)`, a simple line with three nodes would be `LINESTRING (30 10, 10 30, 40 40)`, and a polygon with four nodes would be `POLYGON ((30 10, 40 40, 20 40, 10 20, 30 10))`.

Note that the first and last coordinate pair in a polygon has to be identical.

WKT is a very useful and flexible format. If you are unfamiliar with the concept, you can find a detailed introduction with examples at `http://en.wikipedia.org/wiki/Well-known_text`.

After we've clicked on **OK**, QGIS will prompt us to specify the layer's **coordinate reference system** (**CRS**). We will talk about handling CRS next.

Dealing with coordinate reference systems

Whenever we load a data source, QGIS looks for usable CRS information, for example, in the shapefile's `.prj` file. If QGIS cannot find any usable information, by default, it will ask you to specify the CRS manually. This behavior can be changed by going to **Settings | Options | CRS** to always use either the project CRS or a default CRS.

The QGIS **Coordinate Reference System Selector** offers a filter that makes finding a CRS easier. It can filter by name or ID (for example, the EPSG code). Just start typing and watch how the list of potential CRS gets shorter. There are actually two separate lists; the upper one contains the CRS that we recently used, while the lower list is much longer and contains all the available CRS. For the `elevp.csv` file, we select **NAD27 / Alaska Albers**. With the correct CRS, the `elevp` layer will be displayed as shown in this screenshot:

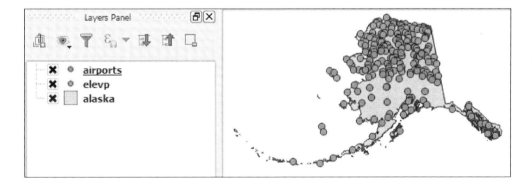

If we want to check a layer's CRS, we can find this information in the layer properties' **General** section, which can be accessed by going to **Layer | Properties** or by double-clicking on the layer name in the layer list. If you think that QGIS has picked the wrong CRS or if you have made a mistake in specifying the CRS, you can correct the CRS settings using **Specify CRS**. Note that this does not change the underlying data or reproject it. We'll talk about reprojecting vectors and raster files in *Chapter 3, Data Creation and Editing*.

In QGIS, we can create a map out of multiple layers even if each dataset is stored with a different CRS. QGIS handles the necessary reprojections automatically by enabling a mechanism called **on the fly reprojection**, which can be accessed by going to **Project | Project Properties**, as shown in the following screenshot. Alternatively, you can click on the **CRS status** button (with the globe symbol and the EPSG code right next to it) in the bottom-right corner of the QGIS window to open this dialog:

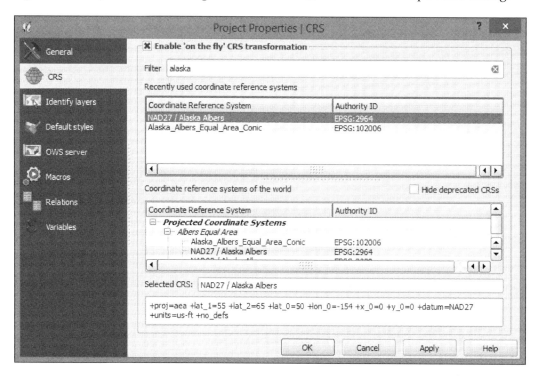

All layers are reprojected to the project CRS on the fly, which means that QGIS calculates these reprojections dynamically and only for the purpose of rendering the map. This also means that it can slow down your machine if you are working with big datasets that have to be reprojected. The underlying data is not changed and spatial analyses are not affected. For example, the following image shows Alaska in its default NAD27 / Alaska Albers projection (on the left-hand side), a reprojection on the fly to WGS84 EPSG:4326 (in the middle), and Web Mercator EPSG:3857 (on the right-hand side). Even though the map representation changes considerably, the analysis results for each version are identical since the on the fly reprojection feature does not change the data.

In some cases, you might have to specify a CRS that is not available in the QGIS CRS database. You can add CRS definitions by going to **Settings | Custom CRS**. Click on the **Add new CRS** button to create a new entry, type in a name for the new CRS, and paste the `proj4` definition string in the **Parameters** input field. This definition string is used by the **Proj4** projection engine to determine the correct coordinate transformation. Just close the dialog by clicking on **OK** when you are done.

 If you are looking for a specific projection `proj4` definition, `http://spatialreference.org` is a good source for this kind of information.

Loading raster files

Loading raster files is not much different from loading vector files. Going to **Layer | Add Layer | Add Raster Layer**, clicking on the **Add Raster Layer** button, or pressing the *Ctrl + Shift + R* shortcut will take you directly to the file-opening dialog. Again, you can check the file type filter to see a list of supported file types.

Let's give it a try and load `landcover.img` from the `raster` sample data folder. Similarly to vector files, you can load rasters by dragging them into QGIS from the operating system or the built-in file browser. The following screenshot shows the loaded raster layer:

 Support for all of these different vector and raster file types in QGIS is handled by the powerful GDAL/OGR package. You can check out the full list of supported formats at www.gdal.org/ formats_list.html (for rasters) and http://www.gdal.org/ ogr_formats.html (for vectors).

Georeferencing raster maps

Some raster data sources, such as simple scanned maps, lack proper spatial referencing, and we have to georeference them before we can use them in a GIS. In QGIS, we can georeference rasters using the **Georeferencer** GDAL plugin, which can be accessed by going to **Raster | Georeferencer**. (Enable it by going to **Plugins | Manage and Install Plugins** if you cannot find it in the **Raster** menu).

The Georeferencer plugin covers the following use cases:

- We can create a world file for a raster file without altering the original raster.
- If we have a map image that contains points with known coordinates, we can set **ground control points (GCPs)** and enter the known coordinates.
- Finally, if we don't know the coordinates of any points on the map, we still have the chance to place GCPs manually using a second, and already georeferenced, map of the same area. We can use objects that are visible in both maps to pick points on the map that we want to georeference and work out their coordinates from the reference map.

After loading a raster into Georeferencer by going to **File | Open raster** or using the **Open raster** toolbar button, we are asked to specify the CRS of the ground control points that we are planning to add. Next, we can start adding ground control points by going to **Edit | Add point**. We can use the pan and zoom tools to navigate, and we can place GCPs by clicking on the map. We are then prompted to insert the coordinates of the new point or pick them from the reference map in the main QGIS window. The placed GCPs are displayed as red circles in both **Georeferencer** and the QGIS window, as you can see in the following screenshot:

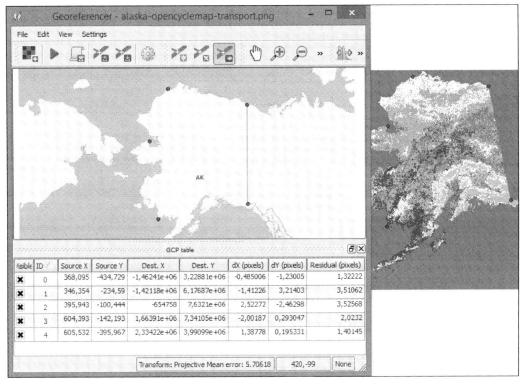

Georeferencer shows a screenshot of the OCM Landscape map © Thunderforest, Data © OpenStreetMap contributors (http://www.opencyclemap.org/?zoom=4&lat=62.50806&lon=-145.01953&layers=0B000)

After placing the GCPs, we can define the transformation algorithm by going to **Settings | Transformation Settings**. Which algorithm you choose depends on your input data and the level of geometric distortion you want to allow. The most commonly used algorithms are polynomial 1 to 3. A **first-order polynomial transformation** allows scaling, translation, and rotation only.

A **second-order polynomial transformation** can handle some curvature, and a **third-order polynomial transformation** consequently allows for even higher degrees of distortion. The **thin-plate spline** algorithm can handle local deformations in the map and is therefore very useful while working with very low-quality map scans. **Projective** transformation offers rotation and translation of coordinates. The **linear** option, on the other hand, is only used to create world files, and as mentioned earlier, this does not actually transform the raster.

The **resampling method** depends on your input data and the result you want to achieve. Cubic resampling creates smooth results, but if you don't want to change the raster values, choose the nearest neighbor method.

Before we can start the georeferencing process, we have to specify the output filename and target CRS. Make sure that the **Load in QGIS when done** option is active and activate the **Use 0 for transparency when needed** option to avoid black borders around the output image. Then, we can close the **Transformation Settings** dialog and go to **File | Start Georeferencing**. The georeferenced raster will automatically be loaded into the main map window of QGIS. In the following screenshot, you can see the result of applying projective transformation using the five specified GCPs:

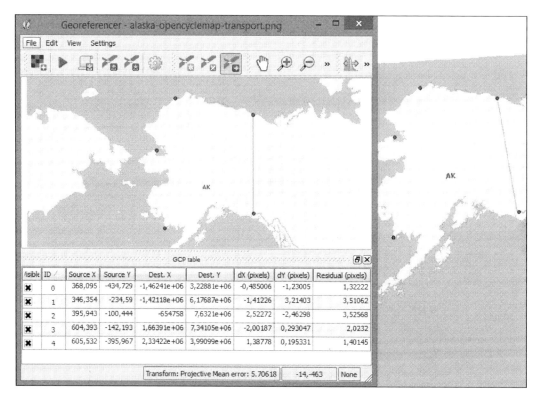

Loading data from databases

QGIS supports **PostGIS**, **SpatiaLite**, **MSSQL**, and **Oracle Spatial** databases. We will cover two open source options: SpatiaLite and PostGIS. Both are available cross-platform, just like QGIS.

SpatiaLite is the spatial extension for SQLite databases. SQLite is a self-contained, server-less, zero-configuration, and transactional SQL database engine (www.sqlite.org). This basically means that a SQLite database, and therefore also a SpatiaLite database, doesn't need a server installation and can be copied and exchanged just like any ordinary file.

You can download an example database from www.gaia-gis.it/spatialite-2.3.1/test-2.3.zip (4 MB). Unzip the file; you will be able to connect to it by going to **Layer | Add Layer | Add SpatiaLite Layer**, using the **Add SpatiaLite Layer** toolbar button, or by pressing *Ctrl + Shift + L*. Click on **New** to select the test-2.3.sqlite database file. QGIS will save all the connections and add them to the drop-down list at the top. After clicking on **Connect**, you will see a list of layers stored in the database, as shown in this screenshot:

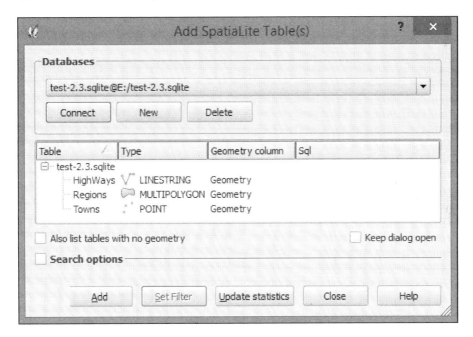

As with files, you can select one or more tables from the list and click on **Add** to load them into the map. Additionally, you can use **Set Filter** to only load specific features.

Filters in QGIS use SQL-like syntax, for example,

`"Name" = 'EMILIA-ROMAGNA'` to select only the region called

`EMILIA-ROMAGNA` or `"Name" LIKE 'ISOLA%'` to select all regions whose names start with `ISOLA`. The filter queries are passed on to the underlying data provider (for example, SpatiaLite or OGR). The provider syntax for basic filter queries is consistent over different providers but can vary when using more exotic functions. You can read the details of OGR SQL at `http://www.gdal.org/ogr_sql.html`.

In *Chapter 4, Spatial Analysis*, we will use this database to explore how we can take advantage of the spatial analysis capabilities of SpatiaLite.

PostGIS is the spatial extension of the PostgreSQL database system. Installing and configuring the database is out of the scope of this book, but there are installers for Windows and packages for many Linux distributions as well as for Mac (for details, visit `http://www.postgresql.org/download/`). To load data from a PostGIS database, go to **Layers | Add Layer | Add PostGIS Layer**, use the **Add PostGIS Layer** toolbar button, or press *Ctrl + Shift + D*.

When using a database for the first time, click on **New** to establish a new database connection. This opens the dialog shown in the following screenshot, where you can create a new connection, for example, to a database called `postgis`:

The fields that have to be filled in are as follows:

- **Name**: Insert a name for the new connection. You can use any name you like.
- **Host**: The server's IP address is inserted in this field. You can use `localhost` if PostGIS is running locally.
- **Port**: The PostGIS default port is `5432`. If you have trouble reaching a database, it is recommended that you check the server's firewall settings for this port.
- **Database**: This is the name of the PostGIS database that you want to connect to.
- **Username** and **Password**: For convenience, you can tell QGIS to save these.

After the connection is established, you can load and filter tables, just as we discussed for SpatiaLite.

Loading data from OGC web services

More and more data providers offer access to their datasets via OGC-compliant web services such as **Web Map Services (WMS)**, **Web Coverage Services (WCS)**, or **Web Feature Services (WFS)**. QGIS supports these services out of the box.

> If you want to learn more about the different OGC web services available, visit `http://live.osgeo.org/en/standards/standards.html` for an overview.

You can load **WMS** layers by going to **Layer | Add WMS/WMTS Layer**, clicking on the **Add WMS/WMTS Layer** button, or pressing *Ctrl + Shift + W*. If you know a WMS server, you can connect to it by clicking on **New** and filling in a name and the URL. All other fields are optional. Don't worry if you don't know of any WMS servers, because you can simply click on the **Add default servers** button to get access information about servers whose administrators collaborate with the QGIS project. One of these servers is called **Lizardtech server**. Select **Lizardtech server** or any of the other servers from the drop-down box, and click on **Connect** to see the list of layers available through the server, as shown here:

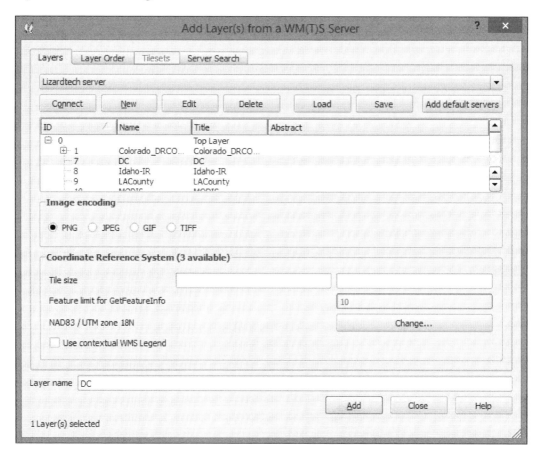

From the layer list, you can now select one or more layers for download. It is worth noting that the order in which you select the layers matters, because the layers will be combined on the server side and QGIS will only receive the combined image as the resultant layer. If you want to be able to use the layers separately, you will have to download them one by one. The data download starts once you click on **Add**. The dialog will stay open so that you can add more layers from the server.

Many WMS servers offer their layers in multiple, different CRS. You can check out the list of available CRS by clicking on the **Change** button at the bottom of the dialog. This will open a CRS selector dialog, which is limited to the WMS server's CRS capabilities.

Loading data from **WCS** or **WFS** servers works in the same way, but public servers are quite rare. One of the few reliable public WFS servers is operated by the city of Vienna, Austria. The following screenshot shows how to configure the connection to the data.wien.gv.at WFS, as well as the list of available datasets that is loaded when we click on the **Connect** button:

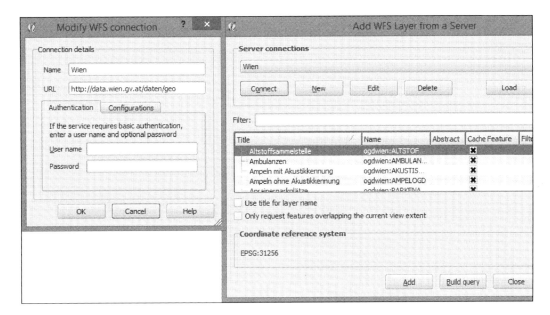

The main advantage of using a **WFS** rather than a **WMS** is that the **Web Feature Service** returns vector features, including all their attributes, instead of only an image of a map. Of course, this also means that WFS layers usually take longer to download and cause more load on the server.

Styling raster layers

After this introduction to data sources, we can create our first map. We will build the map from the bottom up by first loading some background rasters (hillshade and land cover), which we will then overlay with point, line, and polygon layers.

Let's start by loading a land cover and a hillshade from `landcover.img` and `SR_50M_alaska_nad.tif`, and then opening the **Style** section in the layer properties (by going to **Layer | Properties** or double-clicking on the layer name). QGIS automatically tries to pick a reasonable default render type for both raster layers. Besides these defaults, the following style options are available for raster layers:

- **Multiband color**: This style is used if the raster has several bands. This is usually the case with satellite images with multiple bands.

- **Paletted**: This style is used if a single-band raster comes with an indexed palette.

- **Singleband gray**: If a raster has neither multiple bands nor an indexed palette (this is the case with, for example, elevation model rasters or hillshade rasters), it will be rendered using this style.

- **Singleband pseudocolor**: Instead of being limited to gray, this style allows us to render a raster band using a color map of our choice.

The `SR_50M_alaska_nad.tif` hillshade raster is loaded with **Singleband gray Render type**, as you can see in the following screenshot. If we want to render the hillshade raster in color instead of grayscale, we can change **Render type** to **Singleband pseudocolor**. In the pseudocolor mode, we can create color maps either manually or by selecting one of the premade color ramps. However, let's stick to **Singleband gray** for the hillshade for now.

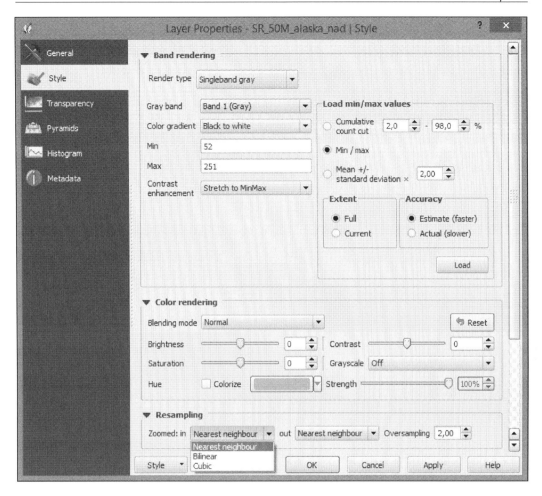

The **Singleband gray** renderer offers a **Black to white Color gradient** as well as a **White to black** gradient. When we use the **Black to white** gradient, the minimum value (specified in **Min**) will be drawn black and the maximum value (specified in **Max**) will be drawn in white, with all the values in between in shades of gray. You can specify these minimum and maximum values manually or use the **Load min/max values** interface to let QGIS compute the values.

Note that QGIS offers different options for computing the values from either the complete raster (**Full Extent**) or only the currently visible part of the raster (**Current Extent**). A common source of confusion is the **Estimate (faster)** option, which can result in different values than those documented elsewhere, for example, in the raster's metadata. The obvious advantage of this option is that it is faster to compute, so use it carefully!

Below the color settings, we find a section with more advanced options that control the raster **Resampling, Brightness, Contrast, Saturation,** and **Hue** — options that you probably know from image processing software. By default, resampling is set to the fast **Nearest neighbour** option. To get nicer and smoother results, we can change to the **Bilinear** or **Cubic** method.

Click on **OK** or **Apply** to confirm. In both cases, the map will be redrawn using the new layer style. If you click on **Apply**, the **Layer Properties** dialog stays open, and you can continue to fine-tune the layer style. If you click on **OK**, the **Layer Properties** dialog is closed.

The landcover.img raster is a good example of a paletted raster. Each cell value is mapped to a specific color. To change a color, we can simply double-click on the **Color** preview and a color picker will open. The style section of a paletted raster looks like what is shown in the following screenshot:

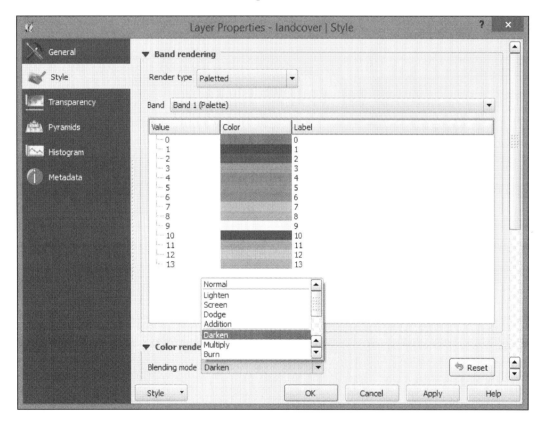

If we want to combine hillshade and land cover into one aesthetically pleasing background, we can use a combination of **Blending mode** and layer **Transparency**. Blending modes are another feature commonly found in image processing software. The main advantage of blending modes over transparency is that we can avoid the usually dull, low-contrast look that results from combining rasters using transparency alone. If you haven't had any experience with blending, take some time to try the different effects. For this example, I used the **Darken** blending mode, as highlighted in the previous screenshot, together with a global layer transparency of **50 %**, as shown in the following screenshot:

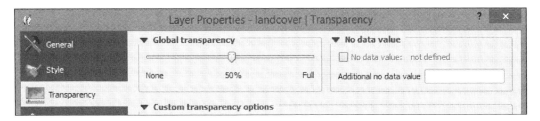

Styling vector layers

When we load vector layers, QGIS renders them using a default style and a random color. Of course, we want to customize these styles to better reflect our data. In the following exercises, we will style point, line, and polygon layers, and you will also get accustomed to the most common vector styling options.

Regardless of the layer's geometry type, we always find a drop-down list with the available style options in the top-left corner of the **Style** dialog. The following style options are available for vector layers:

- **Single Symbol**: This is the simplest option. When we use a **Single Symbol** style, all points are displayed with the same symbol.

- **Categorized**: This is the style of choice if a layer contains points of different categories, for example, a layer that contains locations of different animal sightings.

- **Graduated**: This style is great if we want to visualize numerical values, for example, temperature measurements.

- **Rule-based**: This is the most advanced option. Rule-based styles are very flexible because they allow us to write multiple rules for one layer.

- **Point displacement**: This option is available only for point layers. These styles are useful if you need to visualize point layers with multiple points at the same coordinates, for example, students of a school living at the same address.

- **Inverted polygons**: This option is available for polygon layers only. By using this option, the defined symbology will be applied to the area outside the polygon borders instead of filling the area inside the polygon.

- **Heatmap**: This option is available only for point layers. It enables us to create a dynamic heatmap style.

- **2.5D**: This option is available only for polygon layers. It enables us to create extruded polygons in 2.5 dimensions.

Creating point styles – an example of an airport style

Let's get started with a point layer! Load `airport.shp` from your sample data. In the top-left corner of the **Style** dialog, below the drop-down list, we find the symbol preview. Below this, there is a list of symbol layers that shows us the different layers the symbol consists of. On the right-hand side, we find options for the symbol size and size units, color and transparency, as well as rotation. Finally, the bottom-right area contains a preview area with saved symbols.

Point layers are, by default, displayed using a simple circle symbol. We want to use a symbol of an airplane instead. To change the symbol, select the **Simple marker** entry in the symbol layers list on the left-hand side of the dialog. Notice how the right-hand side of the dialog changes. We can now see the options available for simple markers: **Colors**, **Size**, **Rotation**, **Form**, and so on. However, we are not looking for circles, stars, or square symbols—we want an airplane. That's why we need to change the **Symbol layer type** option from **Simple marker** to **SVG marker**. Many of the options are still similar, but at the bottom, we now find a selection of SVG images that we can choose from. Scroll through the list and pick the airplane symbol, as shown in the following screenshot:

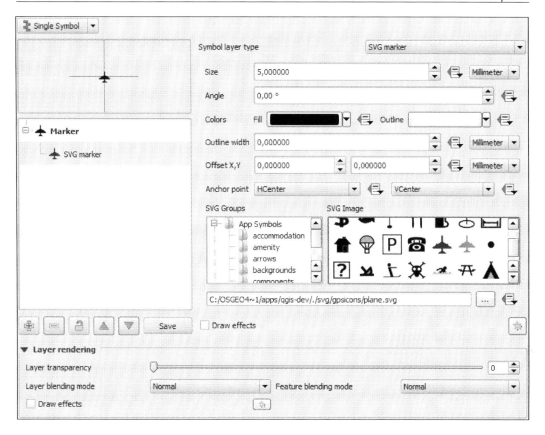

Before we move on to styling lines, let's take a look at the other symbol layer types for points, which include the following:

- **Simple marker**: This includes geometric forms such as circles, stars, and squares

- **Font marker**: This provides access to your symbol fonts

- **SVG marker**: Each QGIS installation comes with a collection of default SVG symbols; add your own folders that contain SVG images by going to **Settings | Options | System | SVG Paths**

- **Ellipse marker**: This includes customizable ellipses, rectangles, crosses, and triangles

- **Vector Field marker**: This is a customizable vector-field visualization tool

- **Geometry Generator**: This enables us to manipulate geometries and even create completely new geometries using the built-in expression engine

Simple marker layers can have different geometric forms, sizes, outlines, and angles (orientation), as shown in the following screenshot, where we create a red square without an outline (using the **No Pen** option):

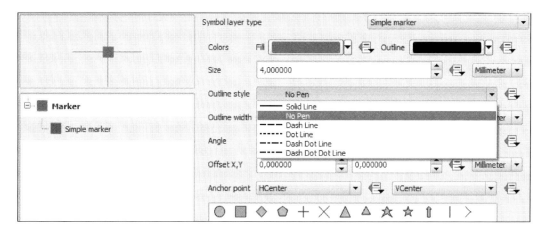

Font marker layers are useful for adding letters or other symbols from fonts that are installed on your computer. This screenshot, for example, shows how to add the yin-and-yang character from the **Wingdings** font:

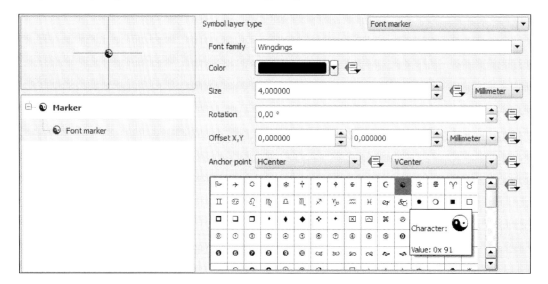

Ellipse marker layers make it possible to draw different ellipses, rectangles, crosses, and triangles, where both the width and height can be controlled separately. This symbol layer type is especially useful when combined with *data-defined overrides*, which we will discuss later. The following screenshot shows how to create an ellipse that is 5 millimeters long, 2 millimeters high, and rotated by 45 degrees:

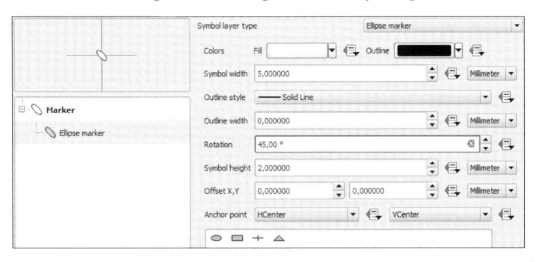

Creating line styles – an example of river or road styles

In this exercise, we create a river style for the `majriver.shp` file in our sample data. The goal is to create a line style with two colors: a fill color for the center of the line and an outline color. This technique is very useful because it can also be used to create road styles.

To create such a style, we combine two simple lines. The default symbol is one simple line. Click on the green **+** symbol located below the symbol layers list in the bottom-left corner to add another simple line. The lower line will be our outline and the upper one will be the fill. Select the upper simple line and change the color to blue and the width to 0.3 millimeters. Next, select the lower simple line and change its color to gray and width to 0.6 millimeters, slightly wider than the other line. Check the preview and click on **Apply** to test how the style looks when applied to the river layer.

You will notice that the style doesn't look perfect yet. This is because each line feature is drawn separately, one after the other, and this leads to a rather disconnected appearance. Luckily, this is easy to fix; we only need to enable the so-called symbol levels. To do this, select the **Line** entry in the symbol layers list and tick the checkbox in the **Symbol Levels** dialog of the **Advanced** section (the button in the bottom-right corner of the style dialog), as shown in the following screenshot. Click on **Apply** to test the results.

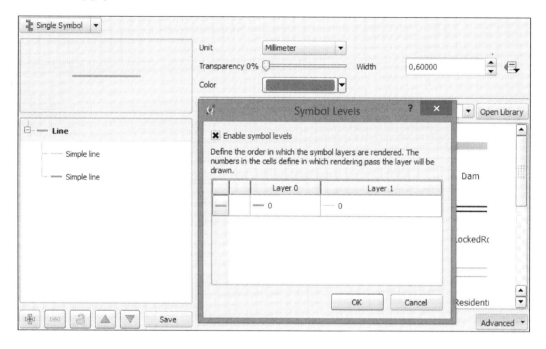

Before we move on to styling polygons, let's take a look at the other symbol layer types for lines, which include the following:

- **Simple line**: This is a solid or dashed line
- **Marker line**: This line is made up of point markers located at line vertices or at regular intervals
- **Geometry Generator**: This enables us to manipulate geometries and even create completely new geometries using the built-in expression engine.

A common use case for **Marker line** symbol layers are train track symbols; they often feature repeating perpendicular lines, which are abstract representations of railway sleepers. The following screenshot shows how we can create a style like this by adding a marker line on top of two simple lines:

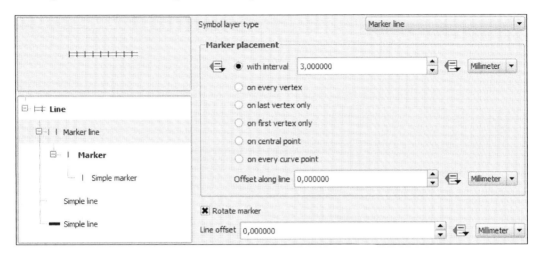

Another common use case for **Marker line** symbol layers is arrow symbols. The following screenshot shows how we can create a simple arrow by combining **Simple line** and **Marker line**. The key to creating an arrow symbol is to specify that **Marker placement** should be **last vertex only**. Then we only need to pick a suitable arrow head marker and the arrow symbol is ready.

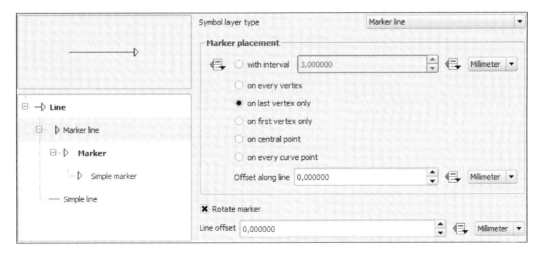

Whenever we create a symbol that we might want to reuse in other maps, we can save it by clicking on the **Save** button under the symbol preview area. We can assign a name to the new symbol, and after we save it, it will be added to the saved symbols preview area on the right-hand side.

Creating polygon styles – an example of a landmass style

In this exercise, we will create a style for the `alaska.shp` file. The goal is to create a simple fill with a blue halo. As in the previous river style example, we will combine two symbol layers to create this style: a **Simple fill** layer that defines the main fill color (white) with a thin border (in gray), and an additional **Simple line** outline layer for the (light blue) halo. The halo should have nice rounded corners. To achieve these, change the **Join style** option of the **Simple line** symbol layer to **Round**. Similar to the previous example, we again enable symbol levels; to prevent this landmass style from blocking out the background map, we select the **Multiply** blending mode, as shown in the following screenshot:

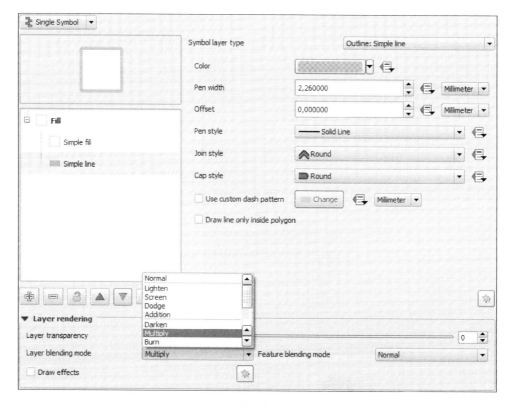

Before we move on, let's take a look at the other symbol layer types for polygons, which include the following:

- **Simple fill**: This defines the fill and outline colors as well as the basic fill styles
- **Centroid fill**: This allows us to put point markers at the centers of polygons
- **Line/Point pattern fill**: This supports user-defined line and point patterns with flexible spacing
- **SVG fill**: This fills the polygon using SVGs
- **Gradient fill**: This allows us to fill polygons with linear, radial, or conical gradients
- **Shapeburst fill**: This creates a gradient that starts at the polygon border and flows towards the center
- **Outline: Simple line** or **Marker line**: This makes it possible to outline areas using line styles
- **Geometry Generator**: This enables us to manipulate geometries and even create completely new geometries using the built-in expression engine.

A common use case for **Point pattern fill** symbol layers is topographic symbols for different vegetation types, which typically consist of a **Simple fill** layer and **Point pattern fill**, as shown in this screenshot:

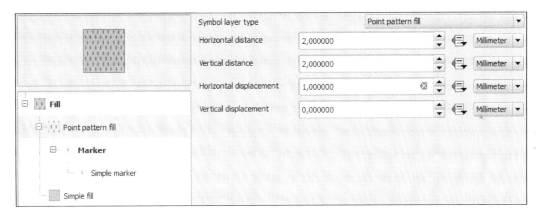

When we design point pattern fills, we are, of course, not restricted to simple markers. We can use any other marker type. For example, the following screenshot shows how to create a polygon fill style with a **Font marker** pattern that shows repeating alien faces from the **Webdings** font:

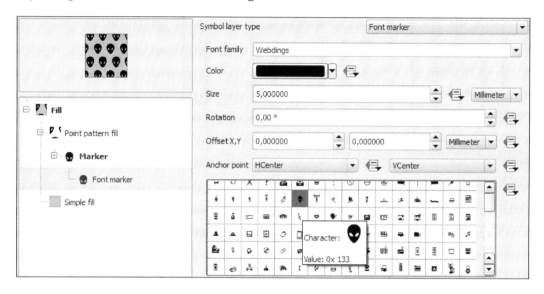

As an alternative to simple fills with only one color, we can create **Gradient fill** symbol layers. Gradients can be defined by **Two colors**, as shown in the following screenshot, or by a **Color ramp** that can consist of many different colors. Usually, gradients run from the top to the bottom, but we can change this to, for example, make the gradient run from right to left by setting **Angle** to 270 degrees, as shown here:

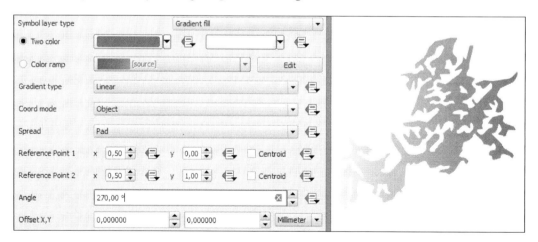

The **Shapeburst fill** symbol layer type, also known as a "buffered" gradient fill, is often used to style water areas with a smooth gradient that flows from the polygon border inwards. The following screenshot shows a fixed-distance shading using the **Shade to a set distance** option. If we select **Shade whole shape** instead, the gradient will be drawn all the way from the polygon border to the center.

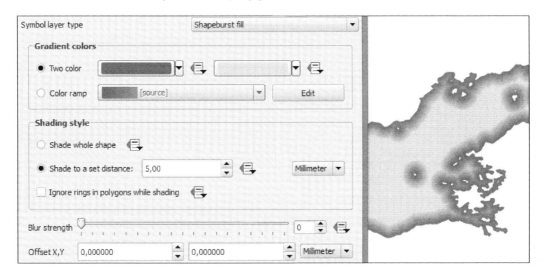

Loading background maps

Background maps are very useful for quick checks and to provide orientation, especially if you don't have access to any other base layers. Adding background maps is easy with the help of the **QuickMapServices** plugin. It provides access to satellite, street, and hybrid maps by different providers.

To install the **QuickMapServices** plugin, go to **Plugins | Manage and Install Plugins**. Wait until the list of available plugins has finished loading. Use the filter to look for the **QuickMapServices** option, as shown in the following screenshot. Select it from the list and click on **Install plugin**. This is going to take a moment. Once it's done, you will see a short confirmation message. You can then close the installer, and the **QuickMapServices** plugin will be available through the **Web** menu.

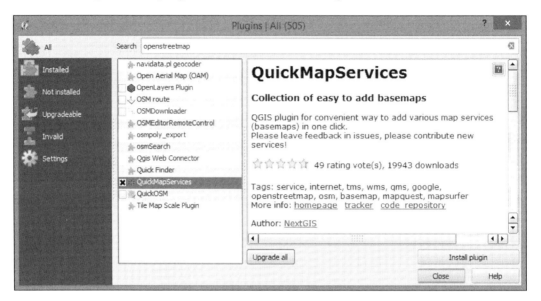

 Note that you have to be online to use these services.

Another fact worth mentioning is that all of these services provide their maps only in Pseudo Mercator (EPSG: 3857). You should change your project CRS to Pseudo Mercator when using background maps from **QuickMapServices**, particularly if the map contains labels that would otherwise show up distorted.

 Background maps added using the **QuickMapServices** plugin are not suitable for printing due to their low resolution.

If you load the **OSM TF Landscape** layer, your map will look like what is shown in this screenshot:

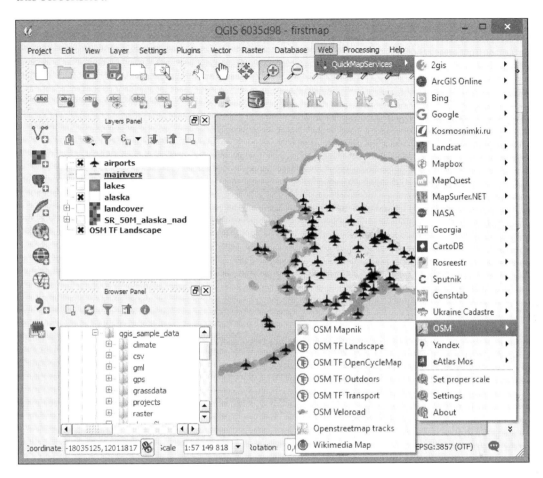

An alternative to the **QuickMapServices** plugin is **OpenLayers Plugin**, which provides very similar functionality but offers fewer different background maps.

Dealing with project files

QGIS project files are human-readable XML files with the filename ending with `.qgs`. You can open them in any text editor (such as **Notepad++** on Windows or **gedit** on Ubuntu) and read or even change the file contents.

When you save a project file, you will notice that QGIS creates a second file with the same name and a `.qgs~` ending, as shown in the next screenshot. This is a simple backup copy of the project file with identical content. If your project file gets *corrupted* for any reason, you can simply copy the *backup* file, remove the ~ from the file ending, and continue working from there.

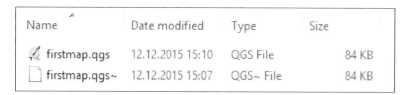

Name	Date modified	Type	Size
firstmap.qgs	12.12.2015 15:10	QGS File	84 KB
firstmap.qgs~	12.12.2015 15:07	QGS~ File	84 KB

By default, QGIS stores the **relative path** to the datasets in the project file. If you move a project file (without its associated data files) to a different location, QGIS won't be able to locate the data files anymore and will therefore display the following **Handle bad layers** dialog:

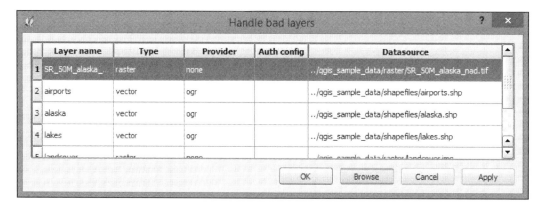

	Layer name	Type	Provider	Auth config	Datasource
1	SR_50M_alaska_	raster	none		../qgis_sample_data/raster/SR_50M_alaska_nad.tif
2	airports	vector	ogr		../qgis_sample_data/shapefiles/airports.shp
3	alaska	vector	ogr		../qgis_sample_data/shapefiles/alaska.shp
4	lakes	vector	ogr		../qgis_sample_data/shapefiles/lakes.shp
5	landcover	raster	none		../qgis_sample_data/raster/landcover.img

 If you are working with data files that are stored on a **network drive** rather than locally on your machine, it can be useful to change from storing **relative paths** to storing **absolute paths** instead. You can change this setting by going to **Project | Project Properties | General**.

To fix the layers, you need to correct the path in the **Datasource** column. This can be done by double-clicking on the path text and typing in the correct path, or by pressing the **Browse** button at the bottom of the dialog and selecting the new file location in the file dialog that opens up.

> A comfortable way to copy QGIS projects to other computers or share QGIS projects and associated files with other users is provided by the **QConsolidate** plugin. This plugin collects all the datasets used in the project and saves them in one directory, which you can then move around easily without breaking any paths.

Summary

In this chapter, you learned how to load spatial data from files, databases, and web services. We saw how QGIS handles coordinate reference systems and had an introduction to styling vector and raster layers, a topic that we will cover in more detail in *Chapter 5, Creating Great Maps*. We also installed our first Python plugin, the QuickMapServices plugin, and used it to load background maps into our project. Finally, we took a look at QGIS project files and how to work with them efficiently. In the following chapter, we will go into more detail and see how to create and edit raster and vector data.

3

Data Creation and Editing

In this chapter, we will first create some new vector layers and explain how to select features and take measurements. We will then continue with editing feature geometries and attributes. After that, we will reproject vector and raster data and convert between different file formats. We will also discuss how to join data from text files and spreadsheets to our spatial data and how to use temporary scratch layers for quick editing work. Moreover, we will take a look at common geometry topology issues and how to detect and fix them, before we end this chapter on how to add data to spatial databases.

Creating new vector layers

In this exercise, we'll create a new layer from scratch. QGIS offers a wide range of functionalities to create different layers. The **New** menu under **Layer** lists the functions needed to create new Shapefile and SpatiaLite layers, but we can also create new database tables using the DB Manager plugin. The interfaces differ slightly in order to accommodate the features supported by each format.

Let's create some new Shapefiles to see how it works:

1. **New Shapefile layer**, which can be accessed by going to **Layer | Create Layer** or by pressing *Ctrl + Shift + N*, opens the **New Vector Layer** dialog with options for different geometry types, CRS, and attributes.

   ° Creating a new Shapefile is really fast because all the mandatory fields already have default values. By default, the tool will create a new point layer in WGS84 (EPSG:4326) CRS (unless specified otherwise in **Settings | Options | CRS**) and one integer field called **id**.

2. Leaving everything at the default values, we can simply click on **OK** and specify a filename. This creates a new Shapefile, and the new point layer appears in the layer list.

3. Next, we also create one line and one polygon layer. We'll add some extra fields to these layers. Besides integer fields (for whole numbers only), Shapefiles also support strings (for text), decimal numbers (also referred to as real), and dates (in ISO 8601 format, that is, 2016-12-24 for Christmas eve 2016).

4. To add a field, we only need to insert a name, select a type and width, and click on **Add to fields list**.

> For decimal numbers, we also have to define the **Precision** value, which determines the number of digits after the comma. A **Length** value of 3 with a **Precision** value of 1 will allow a value range from -99.9 to +99.9.

5. The left-hand side of the following screenshot shows the **New Vector Layer** dialog that was used to create my example polygon layer, which I called `new_polygons`:

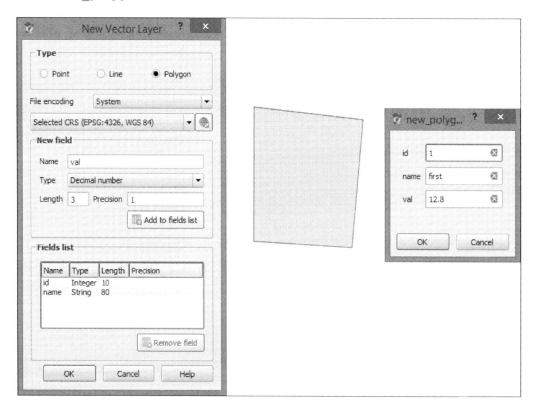

6. All the new layers are empty so far, but we will create some features now. If we want to add features to a layer, we first have to enable editing for that particular layer. Editing can be turned on and off by any one of these ways: going to **Layer | Toggle editing**, using **Toggle editing** in the layer name context menu, or clicking on the **Toggle editing** button in the **Digitizing** toolbar.

> You will notice that the layer's icon in the layer list changes to reflect whether editing is on or off. When we turn on editing for a layer, QGIS automatically enables the digitizing tools suitable for the layer's geometry type.

7. Now, we can use the **Add Feature** tool in the editing toolbar to create new features. To place a point, we can simply click on the map. We are then prompted to fill in the attribute form, which you can see on the right-hand side of the previous screenshot, and once we click on **OK**, the new feature is created.

8. As with points, we can create new lines and polygons by placing nodes on the map. To finish a line or polygon, we simply right-click on the map. Create some features in each layer and then save your changes. We can reuse these test layers in upcoming exercises.

> New features and feature edits are saved permanently only after we've clicked on the **Save Layer Edits** button in the **Digitizing** toolbar, or once we have finished editing and confirmed that we want to save the changes.

Working with feature selection tools

Selecting features is one of the core functions of any GIS, and it is useful to know them before we venture into editing geometries and attributes. Depending on the use case, **selection tools** come in many different flavors. QGIS offers three different kinds of tools to select features using the mouse, an expression, or another layer.

Selecting features with the mouse

The first group of tools in the **Attributes** toolbar allows us to select features on the map using the mouse. The following screenshot shows the **Select Feature(s)** tool. We can select a single feature by clicking on it, or select multiple features by drawing a rectangle. The other tools can be used to select features by drawing different shapes (polygons, freehand areas, or circles) around the features. All features that intersect with the drawn shape are selected.

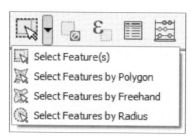

Selecting features with expressions

The second type of select tool is called **Select by Expression**, and it is also available in the **Attribute** toolbar. It selects features based on expressions that can contain references and functions that use feature attributes and/or geometry. The list of available functions in the center of the dialog is pretty long, but we can use the search box at the top of the list to filter it by name and find the function we are looking for faster. On the right-hand side of the window, we find the function help, which explains the functionality and how to use the function in an expression. The function list also shows the layer attribute fields, and by clicking on **all unique** or **10 samples**, we can easily access their content. We can choose between creating a new selection or adding to or deleting from an existing selection. Additionally, we can choose to only select features from within an existing selection. Let's take a look at some example expressions that you can build on and use in your own work:

- Using the `lakes.shp` file in our sample data, we can, for example, select lakes with an area greater than 1,000 square miles by using a simple `"AREA_MI" > 1000.0` attribute query, as shown in the following screenshot. Alternatively, we can use geometry functions such as `$area > (1000.0 * 27878400)`. Note that the `lakes.shp` CRS uses feet, and therefore we have to multiply by 27,878,400 to convert square feet to square miles.

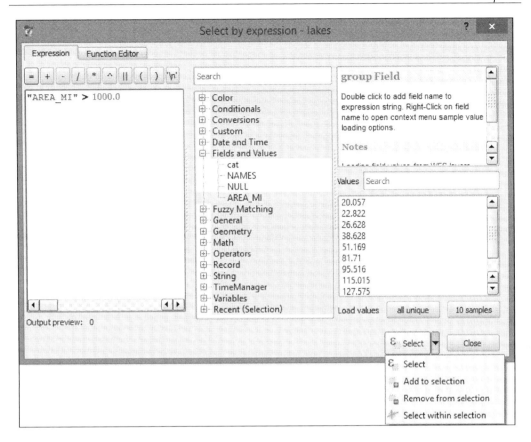

- We can also work with string functions, for example, to find lakes with long names (such as `length("NAMES") > 12`) or lakes with names that contain s or S (such as `lower("NAMES") LIKE '%s%'`); this function first converts the names to lowercase and then looks for any appearance of s.

Selecting features using spatial queries

The third type of tool is called **Spatial Query** and allows us to select features in one layer based on their location relative to features in a second layer. These tools can be accessed by going to **Vector | Research Tools | Select by location** and **Vector | Spatial Query | Spatial Query**. Enable it in **Plugin Manager** if you cannot find it in the **Vector** menu. In general, we want to use the Spatial Query plugin as it supports a variety of spatial operations such as **Crosses**, **Equals**, **Intersects**, **Is disjoint**, **Overlaps**, **Touches**, and **Contains**, depending on the layer geometry type.

Let's test the Spatial Query plugin using `railroads.shp` and `pipelines.shp` from the sample data. For example, we might want to find all railroad features that cross a pipeline; therefore, we select the **railroads** layer, the **Crosses** operation, and the **pipelines** layer. After wc've clicked on **Apply**, the plugin presents us with the query results. There is a list of IDs of the result features on the right-hand side of the window, as you can see in the next screenshot. Below this list, we can check the **Zoom to item** box, and QGIS will zoom into the feature that belongs to the selected ID. Additionally, the plugin offers buttons for direct saving of all the resulting features to a new layer:

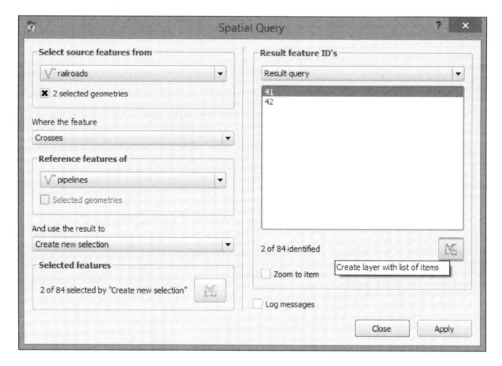

Editing vector geometries

Now that we know how to create and select features, we can take a closer look at the other tools in the **Digitizing** and **Advanced Digitizing** toolbars.

Using basic digitizing tools

This is the basic **Digitizing** toolbar:

The **Digitizing** toolbar contains tools that we can use to create and move features and nodes as well as delete, copy, cut, and paste features, as follows:

- The **Add Feature** tool allows us to create new features by placing feature nodes on the map, which are connected by straight lines.

- Similarly, the **Add Circular String** tool allows us to create features where consecutive nodes are connected by curved lines.

- With the **Move Feature(s)** tool, it is easy to move one or more features at once by dragging them to the new location.

- Similarly, the **Node Tool** feature allows us to move one or more nodes of the same feature. The first click activates the feature, while the second click selects the node. Hold the mouse key down to drag the node to its new location. Instead of moving only one node, we can also move an edge by clicking and dragging the line. Finally, we can select and move multiple nodes by holding down the *Ctrl* key.

- The **Delete Selected**, **Cut Features**, and **Copy Features** tools are active only if one or more layer features are selected. Similarly, **Paste Features** works only after a feature has been cut or copied.

Using advanced digitizing tools

The **Advanced Digitizing** toolbar offers very useful **Undo** and **Redo** functionalities as well as additional tools for more involved geometry editing, as shown in the following screenshot:

The **Advanced Digitizing** tools include the following:

- **Rotate Feature(s)** enables us to rotate one or more selected features around a central point.

- Using the **Simplify Feature** tool, we can simplify/generalize feature geometries by simply clicking on the feature and specifying a desired tolerance in the pop-up window, as shown in the following screenshot, where you can see the original geometry on the left-hand side and the simplified geometry on the right-hand side:

 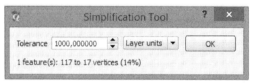 

- The following tools can be used to modify polygons. They allow us to add rings, also known as *holes*, into existing polygons or add parts to them. The **Fill Ring** tool is similar to **Add Ring**, but instead of just creating a hole, it also creates a new feature that fills the hole. Of course, there are tools to delete rings and parts well.

- The **Reshape Features** tool can be used to alter the geometry of a feature by either cutting out or adding pieces. You can control the behavior by starting to draw the new form inside the original feature to add a piece, or by starting outside to cut out a piece, as shown in this example diagram:

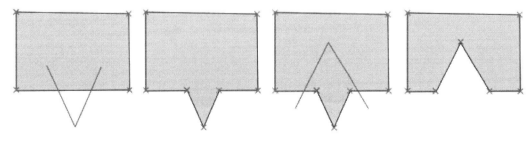

- The **Offset Curve** tool is only available for lines and allows us to displace a line geometry by a given offset.

- The **Split Features** tool allows us to split one or more features into multiple features along a cut line. Similarly, **Split Parts** allows us to split a feature into multiple parts that still belong to the same multipolygon or multipolyline.

- The **Merge Selected Features** tool enables us to merge multiple features while keeping control over which feature's attributes will be available in the output feature.

- Similarly, **Merge Attributes of Selected Features** also lets us combine the attributes of multiple features but without merging them into one feature. Instead, all the original features remain as they were; the attribute values are updated.

- Finally, **Rotate Point Symbols** is available only for point layers with the **Rotation field** feature enabled (we will cover this feature in *Chapter 5, Creating Great Maps*).

Using snapping to enable topologically correct editing

One of the challenges of digitizing features by hand is avoiding undesired gaps or overlapping features. To make it easier to avoid these issues, QGIS offers a **snapping** functionality. To configure snapping, we go to **Settings | Snapping options**. The following screenshot shows how to enable snapping for the **Current layer**. Similarly, you can choose snapping modes for **All layers** or the **Advanced** mode, where you can control the settings for each layer separately. In the example shown in the following screenshot, we enable snapping **To vertex**. This means that digitizing tools will automatically snap to vertices/nodes of existing features in the current layer. Similarly, you can enable snapping **To segment** or **To vertex and segment**. When snapping is enabled during digitizing, you will notice bold cross-shaped markers appearing whenever you go close to a vertex or segment that can be snapped to:

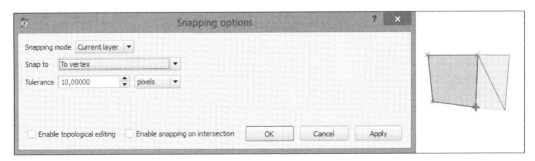

Using measuring tools

Another core functionality of any GIS is provided by **measurement tools**. In QGIS, we find the tools needed to measure lines, areas, and angles in the **Attribute** toolbar, as shown in this screenshot:

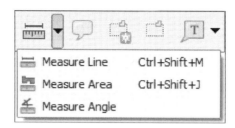

The measurements are updated continuously while we draw measurement lines, areas, or angles. When we draw a line with multiple segments, the tool shows the length of each segment as well as the total length of all the segments put together. To stop measuring, we can just right-click. If we want to change the measurement units from meters to feet or from degrees to radians, we can do this by going to **Settings | Options | Map Tools**.

Editing attributes

There are three main use cases of attribute editing:

- First, we might want to edit the attributes of a specific feature, for example, to fix a wrong name

- Second, we might want to edit the attributes of a group of features

- Third, we might want to change the attributes of all features within a layer

Editing attributes in the attribute table

All three use cases are covered by the functionality available through the **attribute table**. We can access it by going to **Layer | Open Attribute Table**, using the **Open Attribute Table** button present in the **Attributes** toolbar, or in the layer name context menu.

1. To change an attribute value, we always have to enable editing first.

2. Then, we can double-click on any cell in the attribute table to activate the input mode, as shown in the upper dialog of the following screenshot, where I am editing NAME_2 of the first feature:

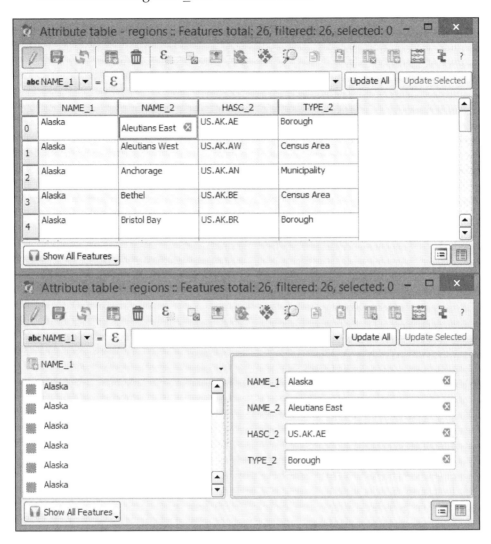

3. Pressing the *Enter* key confirms the change, but to save the new value permanently, we also have to click on the **Save Edit(s)** button or press *Ctrl + S*.

Besides the classic attribute table view, QGIS also supports a **form view**, which you can see in the lower dialog of the previous image. You can switch between these two views using the buttons in the bottom-right corner of the attribute table dialog.

In the attribute table, we also find tools for handling selections (from left to right, starting at the fourth button): **Delete selected features**, **Select features using an expression**, **Unselect all**, **Move selection to top**, **Invert selection**, **Pan map to the selected rows**, **Zoom map to the selected rows**, and **Copy selected rows to clipboard**. Another way to select features in the attribute table is by clicking on the row number.

The next two buttons allow us to add and remove columns. When we click on the **Delete column** button, we get a list of columns to choose from. Similarly, the **New column** button brings up a dialog that we can use to specify the name and data type of the new column.

Editing attributes in the feature form

Another option to edit the attributes of one feature is to open the **attribute form** directly by clicking on the feature on the map using the **Identify tool**. By default, the **Identify tool** displays the attribute values in read mode, but we can enable the **Auto open form** option in the **Identify Results** panel, as shown here:

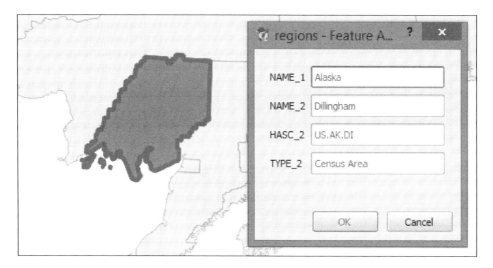

What you can see in the previous screenshot is the default feature attributes form that QGIS creates automatically, but we are not limited to this basic form. By going to **Layer Properties | Fields** section, we can configure the look and feel of the form in greater detail. The **Attribute editor layout** options are (in an increasing level of complexity) **autogenerate**, **Drag and drop designer**, and providing a `.ui` file. These options are described in detail as follows.

Creating a feature form using autogenerate

Autogenerate is the most basic option. You can assign a specific **Edit widget** and **Alias** for each field; this will replace the default input field and label in the form. For this example, we use the following edit widget types:

- **Text Edit** supports inserting one or more lines of text.

- **Unique Values** creates a drop-down list that allows the user to select one of the values that have already been used in the attribute table. If the **Editable** option is activated, the drop-down list is replaced by a text edit widget with autocompletion support.

- **Range** creates an edit widget for numerical values from a specific range.

 For the complete list of available *Edit widget* types, refer to the user manual at `http://docs.qgis.org/2.2/en/ docs/user_manual/working_with_vector/vector_ properties.html#fields-menu`.

Designing a feature form using drag and drop designer

This allows more control over the form layout. As you can see in the next screenshot, the designer enables us to create tabs within the form and also makes it possible to change the order of the form fields. The workflow is as follows:

1. Click on the plus button to add one or more tabs (for example, a **Region** tab, as shown in the following screenshot).

2. On the left-hand side of the dialog, select the field that you want to add to the form.

3. On the right-hand side, select the tab to which you want to add the field.

4. Click on the button with the icon of an arrow pointing to the right to add the selected field to the selected tab.

5. You can reorder the fields in the form using the up and down arrow buttons or, as the name suggests, by dragging and dropping the fields up or down:

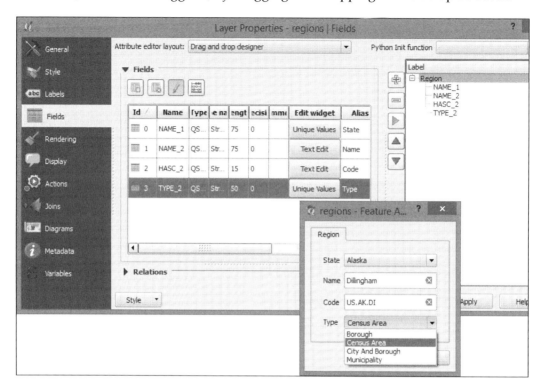

Designing a feature form using a .ui file

This is the most advanced option. It enables you to use a Qt user interface designed using, for example, the Qt Designer software. This allows a great deal of freedom in designing the form layout and behavior.

> Creating .ui files is out of the scope of this book, but you can find more information about it at http://docs.qgis.org/2.2/en/docs/training_manual/create_vector_data/forms.html#hard-fa-creating-a-new-form.

Calculating new attribute values

If we want to change the attributes of multiple or all features in a layer, editing them manually usually isn't an option. This is what the **Field calculator** is good for. We can access it using the **Open field calculator** button in the attribute table, or by pressing *Ctrl + I*. In the **Field calculator**, we can choose to update only the selected features or update all the features in the layer. Besides updating an existing field, we can also create a new field. The function list is the same one that we explored when we selected features by expression. We can use any of the functions and variables in this list to populate a new field or update an existing one. Here are some example expressions that are often used:

- We can create a sequential id column using the @row_number variable, which populates a column with row numbers, as shown in the following screenshot:

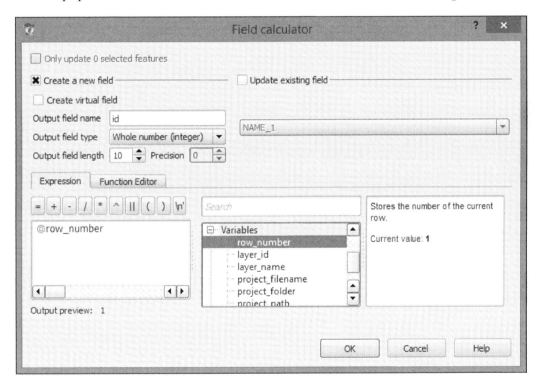

- Another common use case is calculating a line's length or a polygon's area using the $length and $area geometry functions, respectively
- Similarly, we can get point coordinates using $x and $y
- If we want to get the start point or end point of a line, we can use $x_at(0) and $y_at(0), or $x_at(-1) and $y_at(-1), respectively

An alternative to the **Field calculator**—especially if you already know the formula you want to use—is the field calculator bar, which you can find directly in the **Attribute table** dialog right below the toolbar. In the next screenshot, you can see an example that calculates the area of all census areas (use the **New Field** button to add a **Decimal number field** called CENSUSAREA first). This example uses a CASE WHEN – THEN – END expression to check whether the value of TYPE_2 is Census Area:

```
CASE WHEN TYPE_2 = 'Census Area' THEN $area / 27878400 END
```

An alternative solution would be to use the if() function instead. If you use the CENSUSAREA attribute as the third parameter (which defines the value that is returned if the condition evaluates to false), the expression will only update those rows in which TYPE_2 is Census Area and leave the other rows unchanged:

```
if(TYPE_2 = 'Census Area', $area / 27878400,
CENSUSAREA)
```

Alternatively, you can use NULL as a third parameter which will overwrite all rows where TYPE_2 does not equal Census Area with NULL:

```
if(TYPE_2 = 'Census Area', $area / 27878400, NULL)
```

Enter the formula and click on the **Update All** button to execute it:

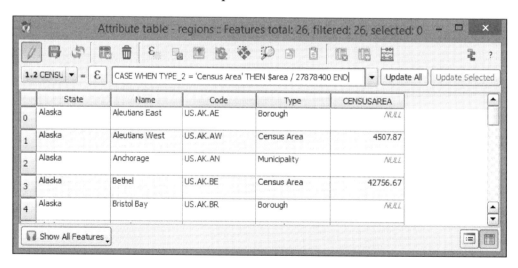

Since it is not possible to directly *change a field data type* in a Shapefile or SpatiaLite attribute table, the field calculator and calculator bar are also used to create new fields with the desired properties and then populate them with the values from the original column.

Reprojecting and converting vector and raster data

In *Chapter 2, Viewing Spatial Data*, we talked about CRS and the fact that QGIS offers on the fly reprojection to display spatial datasets, which are stored in different CRS, in the same map. Still, in some cases, we might want to permanently reproject a dataset, for example, to geoprocess it later on.

In QGIS, reprojecting a vector or raster layer is done by simply saving it with a new CRS. We can save a layer by going to **Layer | Save as...** or using **Save as...** in the layer name context menu. Pick a target file format and filename, and then click on the **Select CRS** button beside the CRS drop-down field to pick a new CRS.

Besides changing the CRS, the main use case of the **Save vector/raster layer** dialog, as depicted in the following screenshot, is conversion between different file formats. For example, we can load a Shapefile and export it as GeoJSON, MapInfo MIF, CSV, and so on, or the other way around.

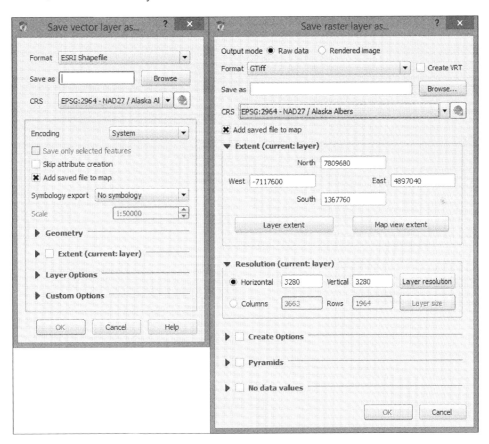

The **Save raster layer** dialog is also a convenient way to clip/crop rasters by a bounding box, since we can specify which **Extent** we want to save.

Furthermore, the **Save vector layer** dialog features a **Save only selected features** option, which enables us to save only selected features instead of all features of the layer (this option is active only if there are actually some selected features in the layer).

 Enabling **Add saved file to map** is very convenient because it saves us the effort of going and loading the new file manually after it has been saved.

Joining tabular data

In many real-life situations, we get additional non-spatial data in the form of spreadsheets or text files. The good news is that we can load XLS files by simply dragging them into QGIS from the file browser or using **Add Vector Layer**. Don't let the wording fool you! It really works without any geometry data in the file. The file can even contain more than one table. You will see the following dialog, which lets you choose which table (or tables) you want to load:

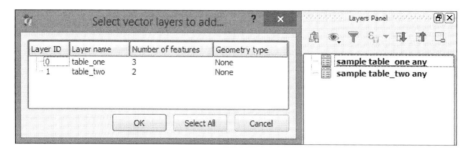

QGIS will automatically recognize the names and data types of columns in an XLS table. It's quite easy to tell because numerical values are aligned to the right in the attribute table, as shown in this screenshot:

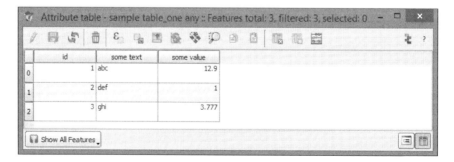

We can also load tabular data from delimited text files, as we saw in *Chapter 2, Viewing Spatial Data*, when we loaded a point layer from a delimited text file. To load a delimited text file that contains only tabular data but no geometry information, we just need to enable the **No geometry (attribute table only)** option.

Setting up a join in Layer Properties

After loading the tabular data from either the spreadsheet or text file, we can continue to join this non-spatial data to a vector layer (for instance, our `airports.shp` dataset, as shown in the following example). To do this, we go to the vector's **Layer Properties | Joins** section. Here, we can add a new join by clicking on the green plus button. All we have to do is select the tabular **Join layer** and **Join field** (of the tabular layer), which will contain values that match those in the **Target field** (of the vector layer). Additionally, we can—if we want to—select a subset of the fields to be joined by enabling the **Choose which fields are joined** option. For example, the settings shown in the following screenshot will add only the `some value` field. Additionally, we use a **Custom field name prefix** instead of using the entire join layer name, which would be the default option.

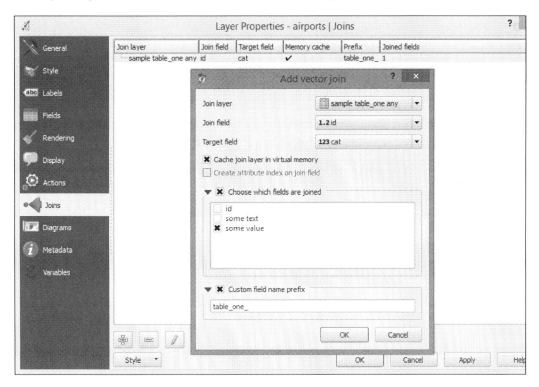

Checking join results in the attribute table

Once the join is added, we can see the extended attribute table and use the new appended attributes (as shown in the following screenshot) for styling and labeling. The way joins work in QGIS is as follows: the join layer's attributes are appended to the original layer's attribute table. The number of features in the original layer is not changed. Whenever there is a match between the join and the target field, the attribute value is filled in; otherwise, you see **NULL** entries.

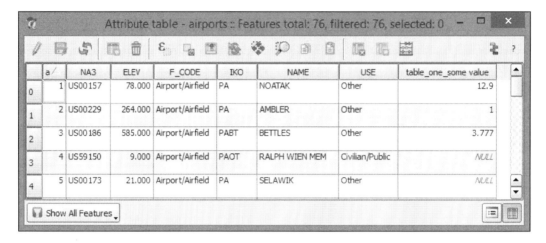

You can save the joined layer permanently using **Save as...** to create the new file.

Using temporary scratch layers

When you just want to quickly draw some features on the map, **temporary scratch layers** are a great way of doing that without having to worry about file formats and locations for your temporary data. Go to **Layer | Create Layer | New Temporary Scratch Layer...** to create a new temporary scratch layer. As you can see in the following screenshot, all we need to do to configure this temporary layer is pick a **Type** for the geometry, a **Layer name**, and a CRS. Once the layer is created, we can add features and attributes as we would with any other vector layer:

As the name suggests, temporary scratch layers are temporary. This means that they will vanish when you close the project.

If you want to preserve the data of your temporary layers, you can either use **Save as...** to create a file or install the **Memory Layer Saver** plugin, which will make layers with memory data providers (such as temporary scratch layers) persistent so that they are restored when a project is closed and reopened. The memory provider data is saved in a portable binary format that is saved with the .mldata extension alongside the project file.

Checking for topological errors and fixing them

Sometimes, the data that we receive from different sources or data that results from a chain of spatial processing steps can have problems. Topological errors can be particularly annoying, since they can lead to a multitude of different problems when using the data for analysis and further spatial processing. Therefore, it is important to have tools that can check data for topological errors and to know ways to fix discovered errors.

Finding errors with the Topology Checker

In QGIS, we can use the **Topology Checker** plugin; it is installed by default and is accessible via the **Vector** menu **Topology Checker** entry (if you cannot find the menu entry, you might have to enable the plugin in **Plugin Manager**). When the plugin is activated, it adds a **Topology Checker Panel** to the QGIS window. This panel can be used to configure and run different topology checks and will list the detected errors.

To see the **Topology Checker** in action, we create a temporary scratch layer with polygon geometries and digitize some polygons, as shown in the following screenshot. Make sure you use snapping to create polygons that touch but don't overlap. These could, for example, represent a group of row houses. When the polygons are ready, we can set up the topology rules we want to check for. Click on the **Configure** button in **Topology Checker Panel** to open the **Topology Rule Settings** dialog. Here, we can manage all the topology rules for our project data. For example, in the following screenshot, you can see the rules we might want to configure for our polygon layer, including these:

- Polygons *must not overlap* each other
- There must not be gaps between polygons
- There shouldn't be any duplicate geometries

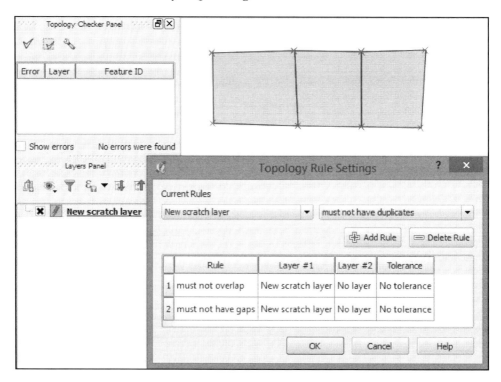

Once the rules are set up, we can close the settings dialog and click on the **Validate All** button in **Topology Checker Panel** to start running the **topology rule** checks. If you have been careful while creating the polygons, the checker will not find any errors and the status at the bottom of **Topology Checker Panel** will display this message: **0 errors were found**. Let's change that by introducing some **topology errors**.

For example, if we move one vertex so that two polygons end up overlapping each other and then click on **Validate All**, we get the error shown in the next screenshot. Note that the error type and the affected layer and feature are displayed in **Topology Checker Panel**. Additionally, since the **Show errors** option is enabled, the problematic geometry part is highlighted in red on the map:

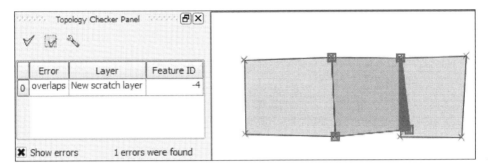

Of course, it is also possible to create rules that describe the relationship between features in different layers. For example, the following screenshot shows a point and a polygon layer where the rules state that each point should be inside a polygon and each polygon should contain a point:

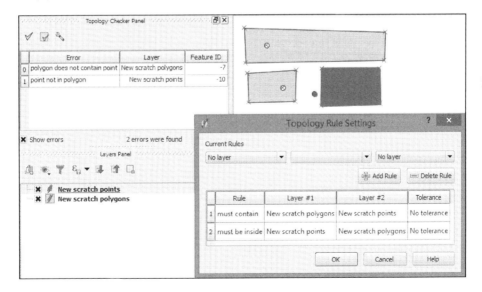

Selecting an error from the list of errors in the panel centres the map on the problematic location so that we can start fixing it, for example, by moving the lone point into the empty polygon.

Fixing invalid geometry errors

Sometimes, fixing all errors manually can be a lot of work. Luckily, certain errors can be addressed automatically. For example, the common error of **self-intersecting polygons**, which cause *invalid geometry* errors (as illustrated in the following screenshot), is often the result of intersecting polygon nodes or edges. These issues can often be resolved using a buffer tool (for example, **Fixed distance buffer** in the **Processing Toolbox**, which we will discuss in more detail in *Chapter 4, Spatial Analysis*) with the buffer **Distance** set to 0. Buffering will, for example, fix the self-intersecting polygon on the left-hand side of the following screenshot by removing the self-intersecting nodes and constructing a valid polygon with a hole (as depicted on the right-hand side):

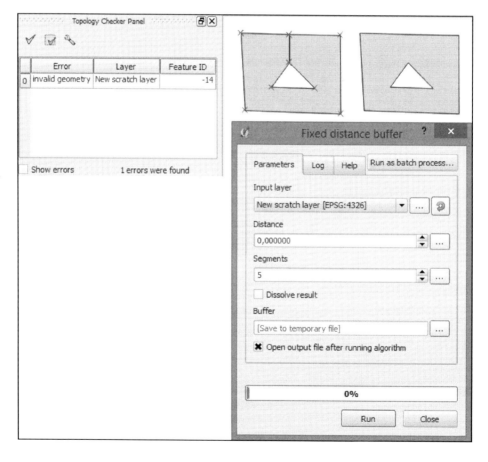

Another common issue that can be fixed automatically is so-called **sliver polygons**. These are small, and often quite thin, polygons that can be the result of spatial processes such as intersection operations. To get rid of these sliver polygons, we can use the **v.clean** tool with the **Cleaning tool** option set to **rmarea** (meaning "remove area"), which is also available through the **Processing Toolbox**. In the example shown in this screenshot, the **Threshold** value of `10000` tells the tool to remove all polygons with an area less than 10,000 square meters by merging them with the neighboring polygon with the longest common boundary:

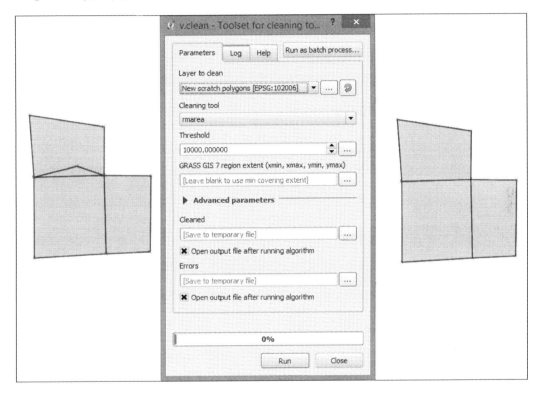

 For a thorough introduction and more details on the **Processing Toolbox**, refer to *Chapter 4, Spatial Analysis*.

Adding data to spatial databases

In *Chapter 2*, *Viewing Spatial Data*, we saw how to view data from spatial databases. Of course, we also want to be able to add data to our databases. This is where the **DB Manager** plugin comes in handy. **DB Manager** is installed by default, and you can find it in the **Database** menu (if **DB Manager** is not visible in the **Database** menu, you might need to activate it in **Plugin Manager**).

The **Tree** panel on the left-hand side of the **DB Manager** dialog lists all available database connections that have been configured so far. Since we have added a connection to the `test-2.3.sqlite` SpatiaLite database in *Chapter 2*, *Viewing Spatial Data*, this connection is listed in **DB Manager**, as shown in the next screenshot.

To add new data to this database, we just need to select the connection from the list of available connections and then go to **Table | Import layer/file**. This will open the **Import vector layer** dialog, where we can configure the import settings, such as the name of the **Table** we want to create as well as additional options, including the input data CRS (the **Source SRID** option) and table CRS (the **Target SRID** option). By enabling these CRS options, we can reproject data while importing it. In the example shown in the following screenshot, we import urban areas from a Shapefile and reproject the data from `EPSG:4326` (WGS84) to `EPSG:32632` (WGS 84 / UTM zone 32N), since this is the CRS used by the already existing tables:

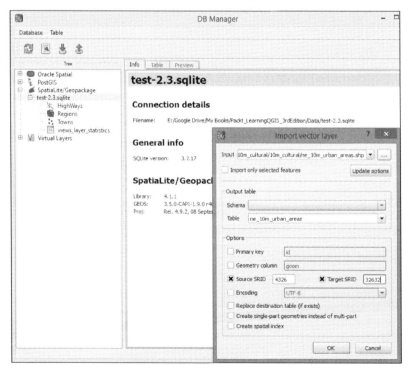

A handy shortcut for importing data into databases is by directly dragging and dropping files from the main window **Browser** panel to a database listed in **DB Manager**. This even works for multiple selected files at once (hold down *Ctrl* on Windows/Ubuntu or *cmd* on Mac to select more than one file in the **Browser** panel). When you drop the files onto the desired database, an **Import vector layer** dialog will appear, where you can configure the import.

Summary

In this chapter, you learned how to create new layers from scratch. We used a selection of tools to create and edit feature geometries in different ways. Then, we went into editing attributes of single features, feature selections, and whole layers. Next, we reprojected both vector and raster layers, and you learned how to convert between different file formats. We also covered tabular data and how it can be loaded and joined to our spatial data. Furthermore, we explored the use of temporary scratch layers and discussed how to check for topological errors in our data and fix them. We finished this chapter with an example of importing new data into a database.

In the following chapter, we will put our data to good use and see how to perform different kinds of spatial analysis on raster and vector data. We will also take a closer look at the **Processing Toolbox**, which has made its first appearance in this chapter. You will learn how to use the tools and combine them to create automated workflows.

4
Spatial Analysis

In this chapter, we will use QGIS to perform many typical geoprocessing and spatial analysis tasks. We will start with raster processing and analysis tasks such as clipping and terrain analysis. We will cover the essentials of converting between raster and vector formats, and then continue with common vector geoprocessing tasks, such as generating heatmaps and calculating area shares within a region. We will also use the Processing modeler to create automated geoprocessing workflows. Finally, we will finish the chapter with examples of how to use the power of spatial databases to analyze spatial data in QGIS.

Analyzing raster data

Raster data, including but not limited to elevation models or remote sensing imagery, is commonly used in many analyses. The following exercises show common raster processing and analysis tasks such as clipping to a certain extent or mask, creating relief and slope rasters from digital elevation models, and using the raster calculator.

Clipping rasters

A common task in raster processing is clipping a raster with a polygon. This task is well covered by the **Clipper** tool located in **Raster | Extraction | Clipper**. This tool supports clipping to a specified **extent** as well as clipping using a polygon **mask** layer, as follows:

- **Extent** can be set manually or by selecting it in the map. To do this, we just click and drag the mouse to open a rectangle in the map area of the main QGIS window.

- A mask layer can be any polygon layer that is currently loaded in the project or any other polygon layer, which can be specified using **Select...**, right next to the **Mask layer** drop-down list.

If we only want to clip a raster to a certain extent (the current map view extent or any other), we can also use the raster **Save as...** functionality, as shown in *Chapter 3, Data Creation and Editing*.

For a quick exercise, we will clip the hillshade raster (SR_50M_alaska_nad.tif) using the Alaska Shapefile (both from our sample data) as a mask layer. At the bottom of the window, as shown in the following screenshot, we can see the concrete gdalwarp command that QGIS uses to clip the raster. This is very useful if you also want to learn how to use **GDAL**.

 In *Chapter 2, Viewing Spatial Data*, we discussed that GDAL is one of the libraries that QGIS uses to read and process raster data. You can find the documentation of gdalwarp and all other GDAL utility programs at http://www.gdal.org/gdal_utilities.html.

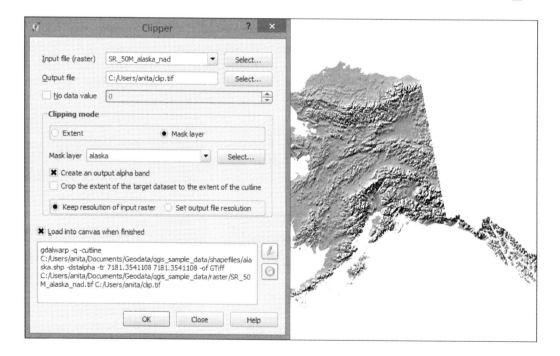

The default **No data value** is the no data value used in the input dataset or **0** if nothing is specified, but we can override it if necessary. Another good option is to **Create an output alpha band**, which will set all areas outside the mask to transparent. This will add an extra band to the output raster that will control the transparency of the rendered raster cells.

A common source of error is forgetting to add the file format extension to the **Output file** path (in our example, `.tif` for GeoTIFF). Similarly, you can get errors if you try to overwrite an existing file. In such cases, the best way to fix the error is to either choose a different filename or delete the existing file first.

The resulting layer will be loaded automatically, since we have enabled the **Load into canvas when finished** option. QGIS should also automatically recognize the alpha layer that we created, and the raster areas that fall outside the Alaska landmass should be transparent, as shown on the right-hand side in the previous screenshot. If, for some reason, QGIS fails to automatically recognize the alpha layer, we can enable it manually using the **Transparency band** option in the **Transparency** section of the raster layer's properties, as shown in the following screenshot. This dialog is also the right place to specify any **No data value** that we might want to be used:

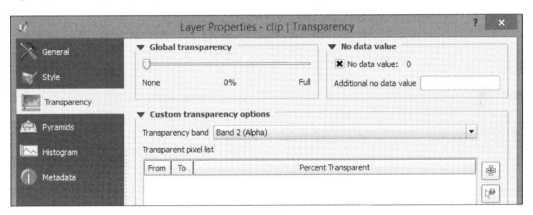

Analyzing elevation/terrain data

To use **terrain analysis tools**, we need an elevation raster. If you don't have any at hand, you can simply download a dataset from the NASA **Shuttle Radar Topography Mission** (**SRTM**) using `http://dwtkns.com/srtm/` or any of the other SRTM download services.

 If you want to replicate the results in the following exercise exactly, then get the dataset called `srtm_05_01.zip`, which covers a small part of Alaska.

Raster **Terrain Analysis** can be used to calculate **Slope**, **Aspect**, **Hillshade**, **Ruggedness Index**, and **Relief** from elevation rasters. These tools are available through the **Raster Terrain Analysis** plugin, which comes with QGIS by default, but we have to enable it in the Plugin Manager in order to make it appear in the **Raster** menu, as shown in the following screenshot:

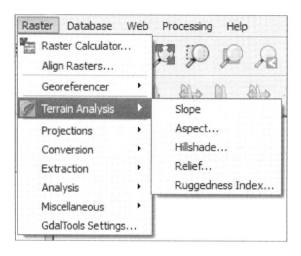

Terrain Analysis includes the following tools:

- **Slope**: This tool calculates the slope angle for each cell in degrees (based on the first-order derivative estimation).

- **Aspect**: This tool calculates the exposition (in degrees and counterclockwise, starting with 0 for north).

- **Hillshade**: This tool creates a basic hillshade raster with lighted areas and shadows.

- **Relief**: This tool creates a shaded relief map with varying colors for different elevation ranges.

- **Ruggedness Index**: This tool calculates the ruggedness of a terrain, which describes how flat or rocky an area is. The index is computed for each cell using the algorithm presented by Riley and others (1999) by summarizing the elevation changes within a 3 x 3 cell grid.

 The results of terrain analysis steps depend on the resolution of the input elevation data. It is recommendable to use small scale elevation data, with for example, 30 meters x/y resolution, particularly when computing ruggedness.

An important element in all terrain analysis tools is the **Z factor**. The Z factor is used if the x/y units are different from the z (elevation) unit. For example, if we try to create a relief from elevation data where x/y are in degrees and z is in meters, the resulting relief will look grossly exaggerated. The values for the z factor are as follows:

- If x/y and z are either all in meters or all in feet, use the default z factor, 1.0

- If x/y are in degrees and z is in feet, use the z factor 370,400

- If x/y are in degrees and z is in meters, use the z factor 111,120

Since the SRTM rasters are provided in WGS84 EPSG:4326, we need to use a **Z factor** of 111,120 in our exercise. Let's create a relief! The tool can calculate relief color ranges automatically; we just need to click on **Create automatically**, as shown in the following screenshot. Of course, we can still edit the elevation ranges' upper and lower bounds as well as the colors by double-clicking on the respective list entry:

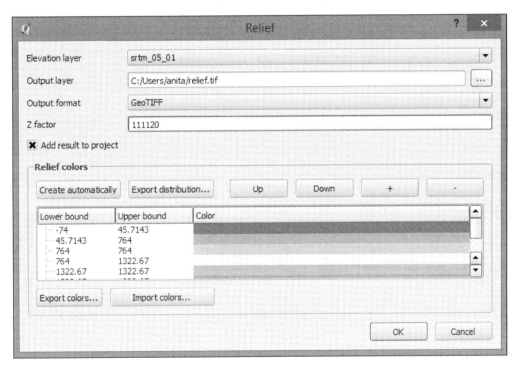

While relief maps are three-banded rasters, which are primarily used for visualization purposes, slope rasters are a common intermediate step in spatial analysis workflows. We will now create a slope raster that we can use in our example workflow through the following sections. The resulting slope raster will be loaded in grayscale automatically, as shown in this screenshot:

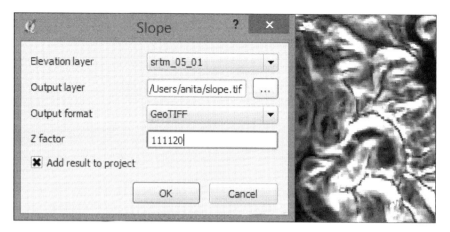

Using the raster calculator

With the **Raster calculator**, we can create a new raster layer based on the values in one or more rasters that are loaded in the current QGIS project. To access it, go to **Raster | Raster Calculator**. All available raster bands are presented in a list in the top-left corner of the dialog using the `raster_name@band_number` format.

Continuing from our previous exercise in which we created a slope raster, we can, for example, find areas at elevations above 1,000 meters and with a slope of less than 5 degrees using the following expression:

```
"srtm_05_01@1" > 1000 AND "slope@1" < 5
```

> You might have to adjust the values depending on the dataset you are using. Check out the *Accessing raster and vector layer statistics* section later in this chapter to learn how to find the minimum and maximum values in your raster.

Cells that meet both criteria of high elevation and evenness will be assigned a value of 1 in the resulting raster, while cells that fail to meet even one criterion will be set to 0. The only bigger areas with a value of 1 are found in the southern part of the raster layer. You can see a section of the resulting raster (displayed in black over the relief layer) to the right-hand side of the following screenshot:

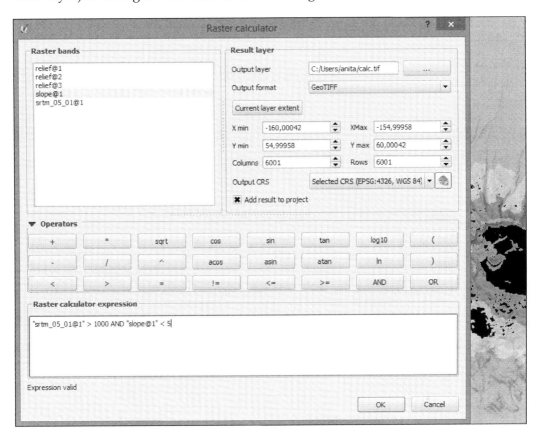

Another typical use case is reclassifying a raster. For example, we might want to reclassify the `landcover.img` raster in our sample data so that all areas with a `landcover` class from 1 to 5 get the value 100, areas from 6 to 10 get 101, and areas over 11 get a new value of 102. We will use the following code for this:

```
("landcover@1" > 0 AND "landcover@1" <= 6 ) * 100
+ ("landcover@1" >= 7 AND "landcover@1" <= 10 ) * 101
+ ("landcover@1" >= 11 ) * 102
```

The preceding raster calculator expression has three parts, each consisting of a check and a multiplication. For each cell, only one of the three checks can be true, and true is represented as `1`. Therefore, if a `landcover` cell has a value of `4`, the first check will be true and the expression will evaluate to `1*100 + 0*101 + 0*102 = 100`.

Combining raster and vector data

Some analyses require a combination of raster and vector data. In the following exercises, we will use both raster and vector datasets to explain how to convert between these different data types, how to access layer and zonal statistics, and finally how to create a raster heatmap from points.

Converting between rasters and vectors

Tools for converting between raster and vector formats can be accessed by going to **Raster | Conversion**. These tools are called **Rasterize (Vector to raster)** and **Polygonize (Raster to vector)**. Like the raster clipper tool that we used before, these tools are also based on **GDAL** and display the command at the bottom of the dialog.

Polygonize converts a raster into a polygon layer. Depending on the size of the raster, the conversion can take some time. When the process is finished, QGIS will notify us with a popup. For a quick test, we can, for example, convert the reclassified `landcover` raster to polygons. The resulting vector polygon layer contains multiple polygonal features with a single attribute, which we name `lc`; it depends on the original raster value, as shown in the following screenshot:

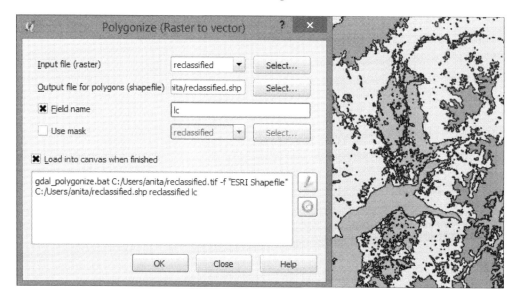

Using the **Rasterize** tool is very similar to using the **Polygonize** tool. The only difference is that we get to specify the size of the resulting raster in pixels/cells. We can also specify the attribute field, which will provide input for the raster cell value, as shown in the next screenshot. In this case, the **cat** attribute of our `alaska.shp` dataset is rather meaningless, but you get the idea of how the tool works:

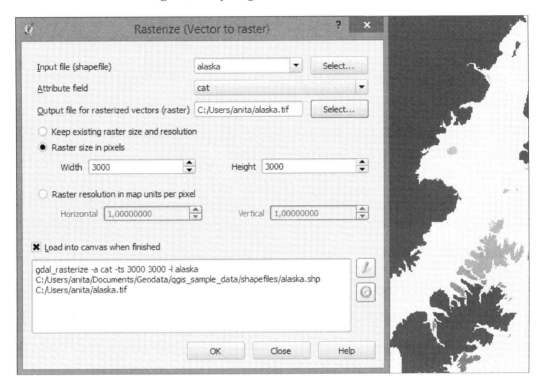

Accessing raster and vector layer statistics

Whenever we get a new dataset, it is useful to examine the layer statistics to get an idea of the data it contains, such as the minimum and maximum values, number of features, and much more. QGIS offers a variety of tools to explore these values.

Raster layer statistics are readily available in the **Layer Properties** dialog, specifically in the following tabs:

- **Metadata**: This tab shows the minimum and maximum cell values as well as the mean and the standard deviation of the cell values.

- **Histogram**: This tab presents the distribution of raster values. Use the mouse to zoom into the histogram to see the details. For example, the following screenshot shows the zoomed-in version of the histogram for our `landcover` dataset:

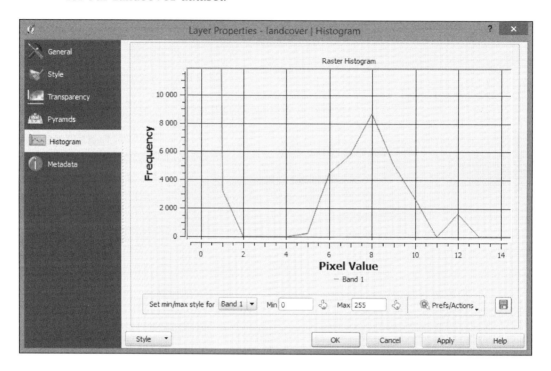

For **vector layers**, we can get summary statistics using two tools in **Vector | Analysis Tools**:

- **Basics statistics** is very useful for numerical fields. It calculates parameters such as mean and median, min and max, the feature count n, the number of unique values, and so on for all features of a layer or for selected features only.

- **List unique values** is useful for getting all unique values of a certain field.

In both tools, we can easily copy the results using *Ctrl + C* and paste them in a text file or spreadsheet. The following image shows examples of exploring the contents of our `airports` sample dataset:

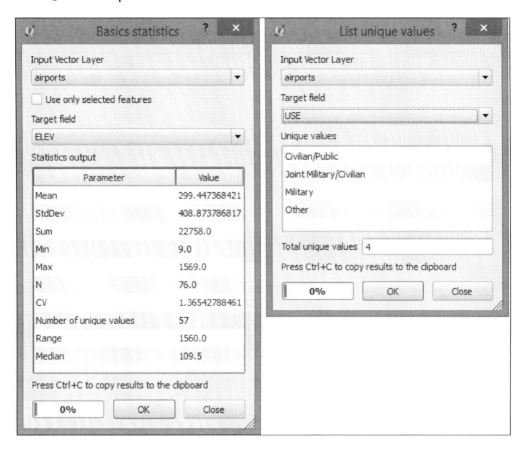

An alternative to the **Basics statistics** tool is the **Statistics Panel**, which you can activate by going to **View | Panels | Statistics Panel**. As shown in the following screenshot, this panel can be customized to show exactly those statistics that you are interested in:

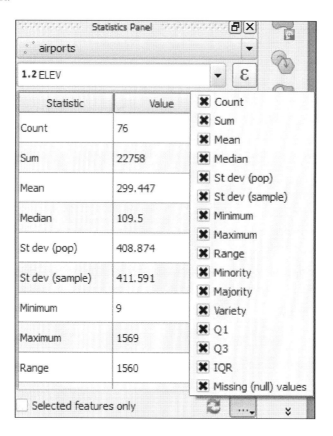

Computing zonal statistics

Instead of computing raster statistics for the entire layer, it is sometimes necessary to compute statistics for selected regions. This is what the **Zonal statistics plugin** is good for. This plugin is installed by default and can be enabled in the **Plugin Manager**.

For example, we can compute elevation statistics for areas around each airport using `srtm_05_01.tif` and `airports.shp` from our sample data:

1. First, we create the analysis areas around each airport using the **Vector | Geoprocessing Tools | Buffer(s)** tool and a buffer size of `10,000` feet.

2. Before we can use the **Zonal statistics plugin**, it is important to notice that the buffer layer and the elevation raster use two different **CRS** (short for **Coordinate Reference System**). If we simply went ahead, the resulting statistics would be either empty or wrong. Therefore, we need to reproject the buffer layer to the raster CRS (WGS84 EPSG:4326, for details on how to change a layer CRS, see *Chapter 3*, *Data Creation and Editing*, in the *Reprojecting and converting vector and raster data* section).

3. Now we can compute the statistics for the analysis areas using the **Zonal Statistics** tool, which can be accessed by going to **Raster | Zonal statistics**. Here, we can configure the desired **Output column prefix** (in our example, we have chosen `elev`, which is short for elevation) and the **Statistics to calculate** (for example, `Mean`, `Minimum`, and `Maximum`), as shown in the following screenshot:

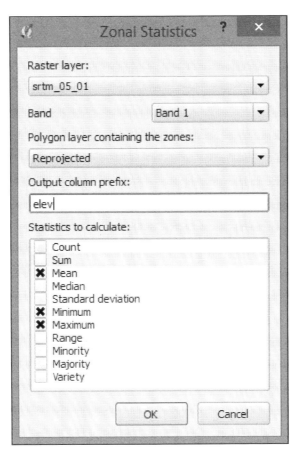

4. After you click on **OK**, the selected statistics are appended to the polygon layer attribute table, as shown in the following screenshot. We can see that **Big Mountain AFS** is the airport with the highest mean elevation among the four airports that fall within the extent of our elevation raster:

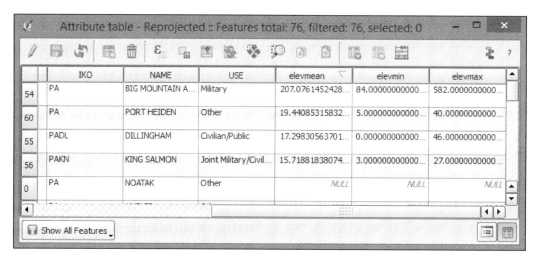

Creating a heatmap from points

Heatmaps are great for visualizing a distribution of points. To create them, QGIS provides a simple-to-use **Heatmap Plugin**, which we have to activate in the **Plugin Manager**, and then we can access it by going to **Raster** | **Heatmap** | **Heatmap**. The plugin offers different **Kernel shapes** to choose from. The kernel is a moving window of a specific size and shape that moves over an area of points to calculate their local density. Additionally, the plugin allows us to control the output heatmap raster size in cells (using the **Rows** and **Columns** settings) as well as the cell size.

Radius determines the distance around each point at which the point will have an influence. Therefore, smaller radius values result in heatmaps that show finer and smaller details, while larger values result in smoother heatmaps with fewer details.

Additionally, **Kernel shape** controls the rate at which the influence of a point decreases with increasing distance from the point. The kernel shapes that are available in the **Heatmap plugin** arc listed in the following screenshot. For example, a Triweight kernel creates smaller hotspots than the Epanechnikov kernel. For formal definitions of the kernel functions, refer to http://en.wikipedia.org/wiki/Kernel_(statistics).

The following screenshot shows us how to create a heatmap of our `airports.shp` sample with a kernel radius of 300,000 layer units, which in the case of our airport data is in feet:

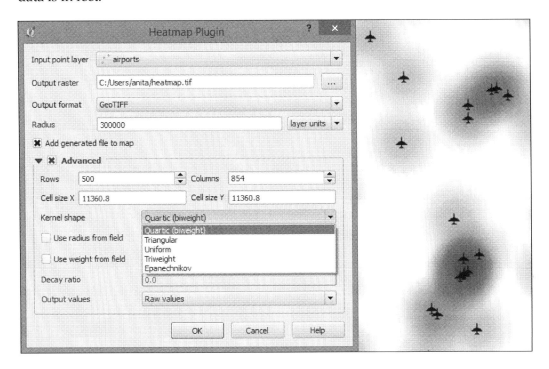

By default, the heatmap output will be rendered using the **Singleband gray** render type (with low raster values in black and high values in white). To change the style to something similar to what you saw in the previous screenshot, you can do the following:

1. Change the heatmap raster layer render type to **Singleband pseudocolor**.

2. In the **Generate new color map section** on the right-hand side of the dialog, select a color map you like, for example, the **PuRd** color map, as shown in the next screenshot.

3. You can enter the **Min** and **Max** values for the color map manually, or have them computed by clicking on **Load** in the **Load min/max values** section.

When loading the raster min/max values, keep an eye on the settings. To get the actual min/max values of a raster layer, enable **Min/max**, **Full Extent**, and **Actual (slower) Accuracy**. If you only want the min/max values of the raster section that is currently displayed on the map, use **Current Extent** instead.

4. Click on **Classify** to add the color map classes to the list on the left-hand side of the dialog.

5. Optionally, we can change the color of the first entry (for value 0) to white (by double-clicking on the color in the list) to get a smooth transition from the white map background to our heatmap.

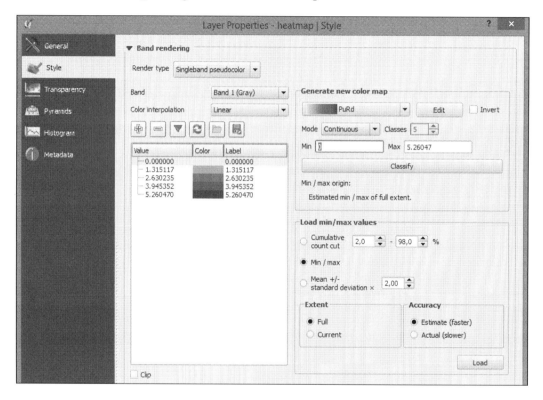

Vector and raster analysis with Processing

The most comprehensive set of spatial analysis tools is accessible via the **Processing plugin**, which we can enable in the **Plugin Manager**. When this plugin is enabled, we find a **Processing** menu, where we can activate the **Toolbox**, as shown in the following screenshot. In the toolbox, it is easy to find spatial analysis tools by their name thanks to the dynamic **Search** box at the top. This makes finding tools in the toolbox easier than in the **Vector** or **Raster** menu. Another advantage of getting accustomed to the Processing tools is that they can be automated in Python and in geoprocessing models.

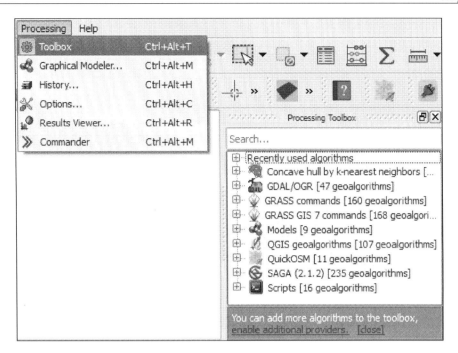

In the following sections, we will cover a selection of the available geoprocessing tools and see how we can use the modeler to automate our tasks.

Finding nearest neighbors

Finding **nearest neighbors**, for example, the airport nearest to a populated place, is a common task in geoprocessing. To find the nearest neighbor and create connections between input features and their nearest neighbor in another layer, we can use the **Distance to nearest hub** tool.

As shown in the next screenshot, we use the populated places as **Source points layer** and the airports as the **Destination hubs layer**. The **Hub layer name attribute** will be added to the result's attribute table to identify the nearest feature. Therefore, we select NAME to add the airport name to the populated places. There are two options for **Output shape type**:

- **Point**: This option creates a point output layer with all points of the source point layer, with new attributes for the nearest hub feature and the distance to it

- **Line to hub**: This option creates a line output layer with connections between all points of the source point layer and their corresponding nearest hub feature

It is recommended that you use **Layer units** as **Measurement unit** to avoid potential issues with wrong measurements:

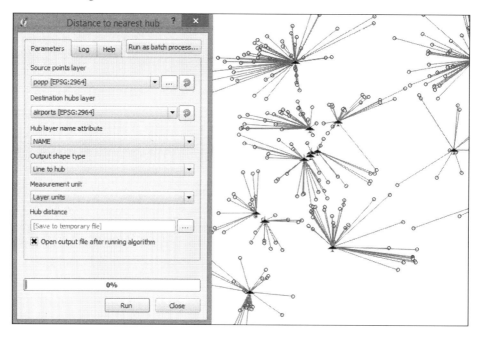

Converting between points, lines, and polygons

It is often necessary to be able to convert between points, lines, and polygons, for example, to create lines from a series of points, or to extract the nodes of polygons and create a new point layer out of them. There are many tools that cover these different use cases. The following table provides an overview of the tools that are available in the Processing toolbox for conversion between points, lines, and polygons:

	To points	**To lines**	**To polygons**
From points		Points to path	Convex hull
			Concave hull
From lines	Extract nodes		Lines to polygons
			Convex hull
From polygons	Extract nodes	Polygons to lines	
	Polygon centroids		
	(Random points inside a polygon)		

In general, it is easier to convert more complex representations to simpler ones (polygons to lines, polygons to points, or lines to points) than conversion in the other direction (points to lines, points to polygons, or lines to polygons). Here is a short overview of these tools:

- **Extract nodes**: This is a very straightforward tool. It takes one input layer with lines or polygons and creates a point layer that contains all the input geometry nodes. The resulting points contain all the attributes of the original line or polygon feature.

- **Polygon centroids**: This tool creates one centroid per polygon or multipolygon. It is worth noting that it does not ensure that the centroid falls within the polygon. For concave polygons, multipolygons, and polygons with holes, the centroid can therefore fall outside the polygon.

- **Random points inside polygon**: This tool creates a certain number of points at random locations inside the polygon.

- **Points to path**: To be able to create lines from points, the point layer needs attributes that identify the line (**Group field**) and the order of points in the line (**Order field**), as shown in this screenshot:

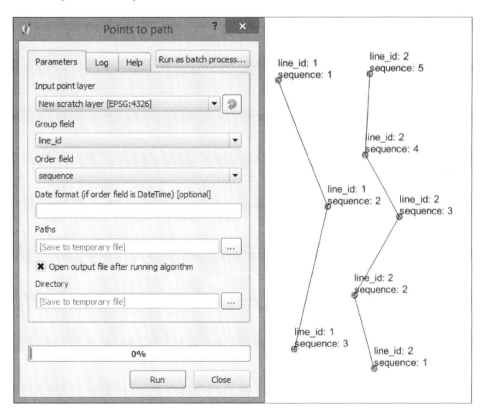

- **Convex hull**: This tool creates a convex hull around the input points or lines. The convex hull can be imagined as an area that contains all the input points as well as all the connections between the input points.

- **Concave hull**: This tool creates a concave hull around the input points. The concave hull is a polygon that represents the area occupied by the input points. The concave hull is equal to or smaller than the convex hull. In this tool, we can control the level of detail of the concave hull by changing the **Threshold** parameter between 0 (very detailed) and 1 (which is equivalent to the convex hull). The following screenshot shows a comparison between convex and concave hulls (with the threshold set to 0.3) around our airport data:

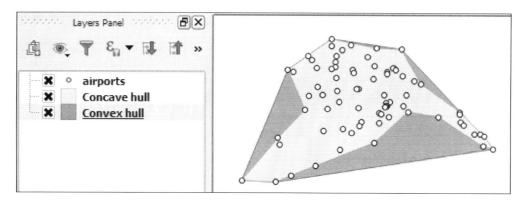

- **Lines to polygon**: Finally, this tool can create polygons from lines that enclose an area. Make sure that there are no gaps between the lines. Otherwise, it will not work.

Identifying features in the proximity of other features

One common spatial analysis task is to identify features in the proximity of certain other features. One example would be to find all airports near rivers. Using airports.shp and majrivers.shp from our sample data, we can find airports within 5,000 feet of a river by using a combination of the **Fixed distance buffer** and **Select by location** tools. Use the search box to find the tools in the Processing Toolbox. The tool configurations for this example are shown in the following screenshot:

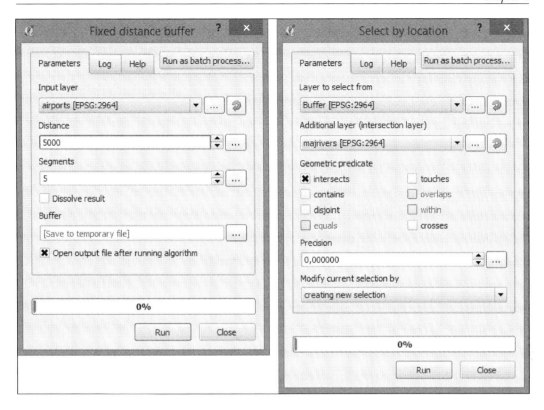

After buffering the airport point locations, the **Select by location** tool selects all the airport buffers that intersect a river. As a result, 14 out of the 76 airports are selected. This information is displayed in the information area at the bottom of the QGIS main window, as shown in this screenshot:

14 feature(s) selected on layer Buffer.

If you ever forget which settings you used or need to check whether you have used the correct input layer, you can go to **Processing | History**. The **ALGORITHM** section lists all the algorithms that we have been running as well as the used settings, as shown in the following screenshot:

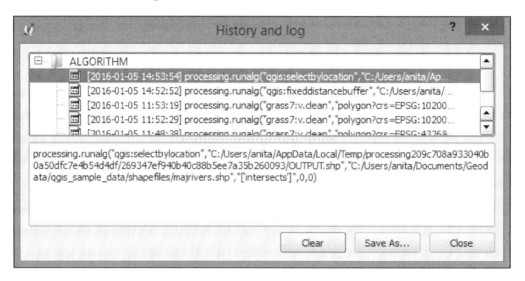

The commands listed under **ALGORITHM** can also be used to call Processing tools from the QGIS Python console, which can be activated by going to **Plugins | Python Console**. The Python commands shown in the following screenshot run the buffer algorithm (`processing.runalg`) and load the result into the map (`processing.load`):

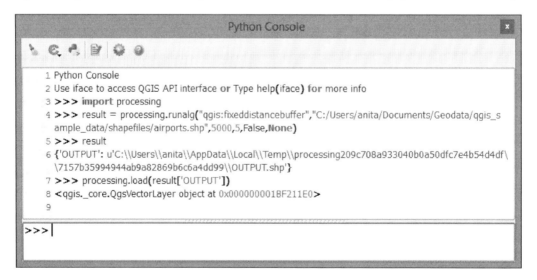

Sampling a raster at point locations

Another common task is to sample a raster at specific point locations. Using Processing, we can solve this problem with a **GRASS** tool called v.sample. To use GRASS tools, make sure that GRASS is installed and Processing is configured correctly under **Processing | Options and configuration**. On an OSGeo4W default system, the configuration will look like what is shown here:

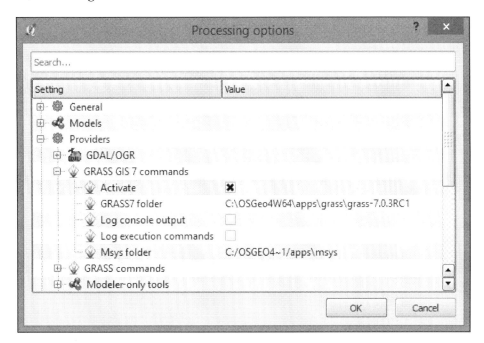

At the time of writing this book, GRASS 7.0.3RC1 is available in OSGeo4W. As shown in the previous screenshot, there is also support for the previous GRASS version 6.x, and Processing can be configured to use its algorithms as well. In the toolbox, you will find the algorithms under **GRASS GIS 7 commands** and **GRASS commands** (for GRASS 6.x).

For this exercise, let's imagine we want to sample the **landcover** layer at the airport locations of our sample data. All we have to do is specify the vector layer containing the sample points and the raster layer that should be sampled. For this example, we can leave all other settings at their default values, as shown in the following screenshot. The tool not only samples the raster but also compares point attributes with the sampled raster value. However, we don't need this comparison in our current example:

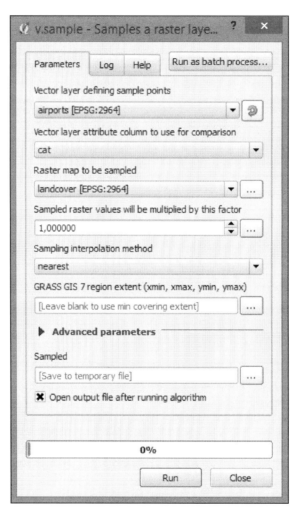

Mapping density with hexagonal grids

Mapping the density of points using a hexagonal grid has become quite a popular alternative to creating heatmaps. Processing offers us a fast way to create such an analysis. There is already a pre-made script called **Hex grid from layer bounds**, which is available through the Processing scripts collection and can be downloaded using the **Get scripts from on-line scripts collection** tool. As you can see in the following screenshot, you just need to enable the script by ticking the checkbox and clicking OK:

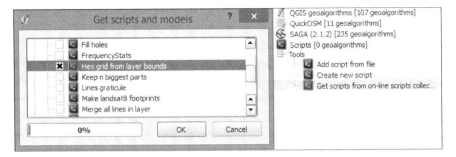

Then, we can use this script to create a hexagonal grid that covers all points in the input layer. The dataset of populated places (popp.shp), is a good sample dataset for this exercise. Once the grid is ready, we can run **Count points in polygon** to calculate the statistics. The number of points will be stored in the **NUMPOINTS** column if you use the settings shown in the following screenshot:

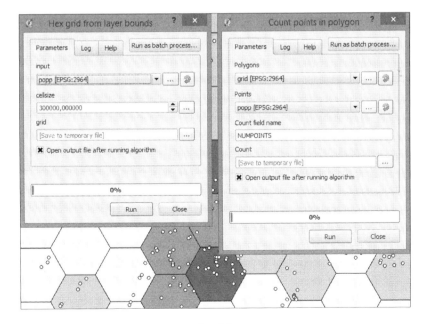

Calculating area shares within a region

Another spatial analysis task we often encounter is calculating area shares within a certain region, for example, landcover shares along one specific river. Using `majrivers.shp` and `trees.shp`, we can calculate the share of wooded area in a 10,000-foot-wide strip of land along the Susitna River:

1. We first define the analysis region by selecting the river and buffering it.

 QGIS Processing will only apply buffers to the selected features of the input layer. This default behavior can be changed under **Processing | Options and configuration** by disabling the **Use only selected features** option. For the following examples, please leave the option enabled.

To select the Susitna River, we use the **Select by attribute** tool. After running the tool, you should see that our river of interest is selected and highlighted.

2. Then we can use the **Fixed distance buffer** tool to get the area within 5,000 feet along the river. Note that the **Dissolve result** option should be enabled to ensure that the buffer result is one continuous polygon, as shown in the following screenshot:

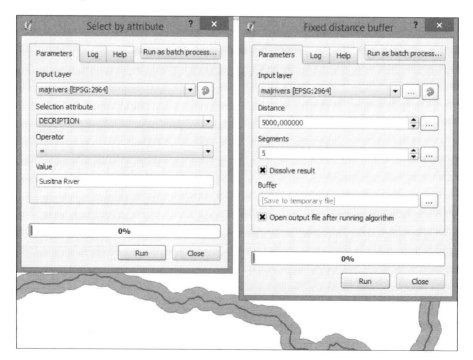

3. Next, we calculate the size of the strip of land around our river. This can be done using the **Export/Add geometry columns** tool, which adds the area and perimeter to the attribute table.

4. Then, we can calculate the **Intersection** between the area along the river and the wooded areas in `trees.shp`, as shown in the following screenshot. The result of this operation is a layer that contains only those wooded areas within the river buffer.

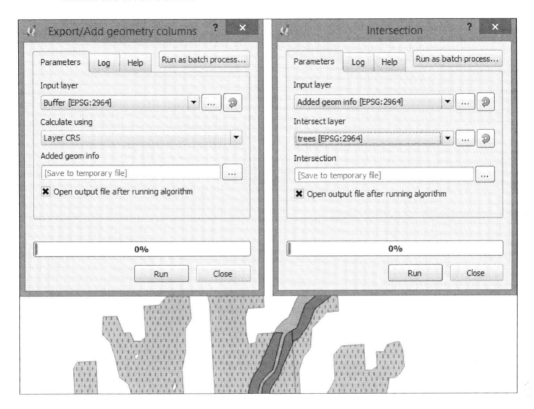

5. Using the **Dissolve** tool, we can recombine all areas from the intersection results into one big polygon that represents the total wooded area around the river. Note how we use the **Unique ID field** VEGDESC to only combine areas with the same vegetation in order not to mix deciduous and mixed trees.

6. Finally, we can calculate the final share of wooded area using the **Advanced Python field calculator**. The formula `value = $geom.area()/<area>` divides the area of the final polygon (`$geom.area()`) by the value in the `area` attribute (`<area>`), which we created earlier by running **Export/Add geometry columns**. As shown in the following screenshot, this calculation results in a wood share of **0.31601** for **Deciduous** and **0.09666** for **Mixed Trees**. Therefore, we can conclude that in total, 41.27 percent of the land along the Susitna River is wooded:

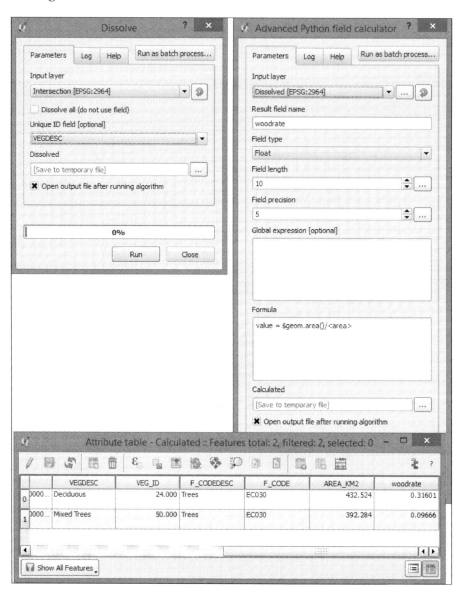

Batch-processing multiple datasets

Sometimes, we want to run the same tool repeatedly but with slightly different settings. For this use case, **Processing** offers the **Batch Processing** functionality. Let's use this tool to extract some samples from our airports layer using the **Random extract** tool:

1. To access the batch processing functionality, right-click on the **Random extract** tool in the toolbox and select **Execute as batch process**. This will open the **Batch Processing** dialog.

2. Next, we configure the **Input layer** by clicking on the **...** button and selecting **Select from open layers**, as shown in the following screenshot:

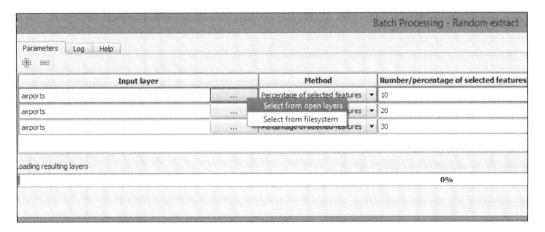

3. This will open a small dialog in which we can select the `airports` layer and click on **OK**.

4. To automatically fill in the other rows with the same input layer, we can double-click on the table header of the corresponding column (which reads **Input layer**).

5. Next, we configure the **Method** by selecting the **Percentage of selected features** option and again double-clicking on the respective table header to auto-fill the remaining rows.

6. The next parameter controls the **Number/percentage of selected features**. For our exercise, we configure **10**, **20**, and **30** percent.

7. Last but not least, we need to configure the output files in the **Extracted (random)** column. Click on the **...** button, which will open a file dialog. There, you can select the save location and filename (for example, `extract`) and click on **Save**.

8. This will open the **Autofill settings** dialog, which helps us to automatically create distinct filenames for each run. Using the **Fill with parameter values** mode with the **Number/percentage of selected features** parameter will automatically append our parameter values (**10**, **20**, and **30**, respectively) to the filename. This will result in `extract10`, `extract20`, and `extract30`, as shown in the following screenshot:

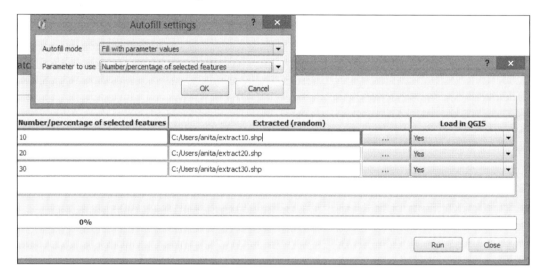

9. Once everything is configured, click on the **Run** button and wait for all the batch instructions to be processed and the results to be loaded into the project.

Automated geoprocessing with the graphical modeler

Using the graphical modeler, we can turn entire geoprocessing and analysis workflows into automated models. We can then use these models to run complex geoprocessing tasks that involve multiple different tools in one go. To create a model, we go to **Processing | Graphical modeler** to open the modeler, where we can select from different **Inputs** and **Algorithms** for our model.

Let's create a model that automates the creation of hexagonal heatmaps!

1. By double-clicking on the **Vector layer** entry in the **Inputs** list, we can add an input field for the point layer. It's a good idea to use descriptive parameter names (for example, `hex cell size` instead of just `size` for the parameter that controls the size of the hexagonal grid cells) so that we can recognize which input is first and which is later in the model. It is also useful to restrict the **Shape type** field wherever appropriate. In our example, we restrict the input to **Point** layers. This will enable Processing to pre-filter the available layers and present us only the layers of the correct type.

2. The second input that we need is a **Number** field to specify the desired hexagonal cell size, as shown in this screenshot:

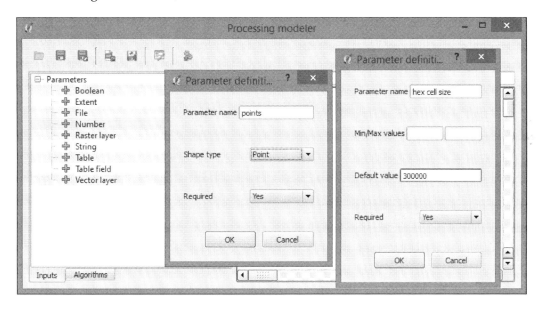

3. After adding the inputs, we can now continue creating the model by assembling the algorithms. In the **Algorithms** section, we can use the filter at the top to narrow down our search for the correct algorithm. To add an algorithm to the model, we simply double-click on the entry in the list of algorithms. This opens the algorithm dialog, where we have to specify the inputs and further algorithm-specific parameters.

4. In our example, we want to use the point vector layer as the **input** layer and the number input **hex cell size** as the **cellsize** parameter. We can access the available inputs through the drop-down list, as shown in the following screenshot. Alternatively, it's possible to hardcode parameters such as the cell size by typing the desired value in the input field:

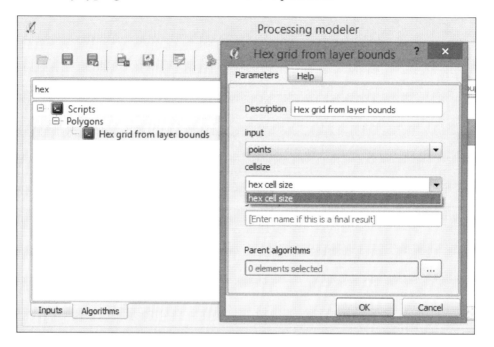

While adding the following algorithms, it is important to always choose the correct input layer based on the previous processing step. We can verify the workflow using the connections in the model diagram that the modeler draws automatically.

5. The final model will look like this:

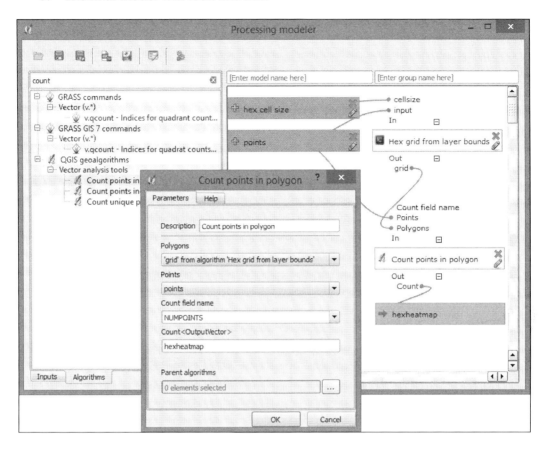

6. To finish the model, we need to enter a model name (for example, `Create hexagonal heatmap`) and a group name (for example, `Learning QGIS`). Processing will use the group name to organize all the models that we create into different toolbox groups. Once we have picked a name and group, we can save the model and then run it.

7. After closing the modeler, we can run the saved models from the toolbox like any other tool. It is even possible to use one model as a building block for another model.

Another useful feature is that we can specify a layer style that needs to be applied to the processing results automatically. This default style can be set using **Edit rendering styles for outputs** in the context menu of the created model in the toolbox, as shown in the following screenshot:

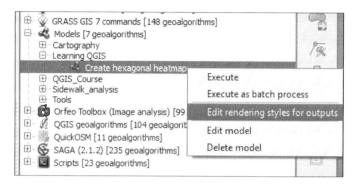

Documenting and sharing models

Models can easily be copied from one QGIS installation to another and shared with other users. To ensure the usability of the model, it is a good idea to write a short documentation. **Processing** provides a convenient **Help editor**; it can be accessed by clicking on the **Edit model help** button in the **Processing modeler**, as shown in this screenshot:

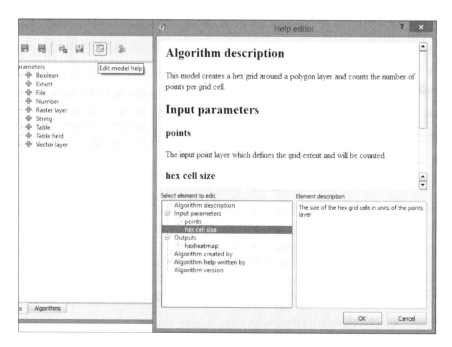

By default, the `.model` files are stored in your user directory. On Windows, it is `C:\Users\<your_user_name>\.qgis2\processing\models`, and on Linux and OS X, it is `~/.qgis2/processing/models`.

You can copy these files and share them with others. To load a model from a file, use the loading tool by going to **Models** | **Tools** | **Add model from file** in the **Processing Toolbox**.

Leveraging the power of spatial databases

Another approach to geoprocessing is to use the functionality provided by spatial databases such as PostGIS and SpatiaLite. In the *Loading data from databases* section of *Chapter 2, Viewing Spatial Data*, we discussed how to load data from a SpatiaLite database. In this exercise, we will use SpatiaLite's built-in geoprocessing functions to perform spatial analysis directly in the database and visualize the results in QGIS. We will use the same SpatiaLite database that we downloaded in *Chapter 2, Viewing Spatial Data*, from `www.gaia-gis.it/spatialite-2.3.1/test-2.3.zip` (4 MB).

Selecting by location in SpatiaLite

As an example, we will use SpatiaLite's spatial functions to get all highways that are within 1 km distance from the city of Firenze:

1. To interact with the database, we use the **DB Manager** plugin, which can be enabled in the **Plugin Manager** and is available via the **Database** menu.

    If you have followed the *Loading data from databases* section in *Chapter 2, Viewing Spatial Data*, you will see `test-2.3.sqlite` listed under SpatiaLite in the tree on the left-hand side of the **DB Manager** dialog, as shown in the next screenshot. If the database is not listed, refer to the previously mentioned section to set up the database connection.

2. Next, we can open a **Query** tab using the **SQL window** toolbar button, by going to **Database** | **SQL window**, or by pressing *F2*. The following **SQL** query will select all highways that are within 1 km distance from the city of Firenze:

    ```
    SELECT *
    FROM HighWays
    WHERE PtDistWithin(
      HighWays.Geometry,
    ```

```
(SELECT Geometry FROM Towns WHERE Name = 'Firenze'),
1000
)
```

The `SELECT Geometry FROM Towns WHERE Name = 'Firenze'` subquery selects the point geometry that represents the city of Firenze. This point is then used in the `PtDistWithin` function to test for each highway geometry and check whether it is within a distance of 1,000 meters.

An introduction to SQL is out of the scope of this book, but you can find a thorough tutorial on using SpatiaLite at `http://www.gaia-gis.it/gaia-sins/spatialite-cookbook/index.html`. Additionally, to get an overview of all the spatial functionalities offered by SpatiaLite, visit `http://www.gaia-gis.it/gaia-sins/spatialite-sql-4.2.0.html`.

3. When the query is entered, we can click on **Execute (F5)** to run the query. The query results will be displayed in a tabular form in the result section below the SQL query input area, as shown in the following screenshot:

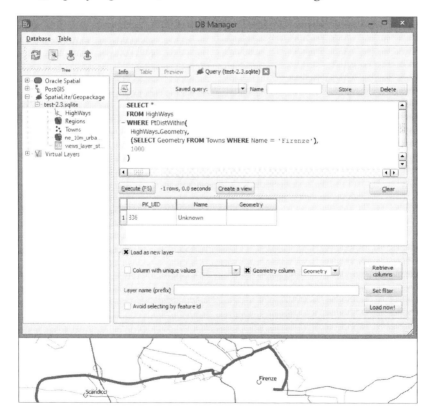

4. To display the query results on the map, we need to activate the **Load as new layer** option below the results table. Make sure you select the correct **Geometry column** (Geometry).

5. Once you have configured these settings, you can click on **Load now!** to load the query result as a new map layer. As you can see in the preceding screenshot, only one of the highways (represented by the wide blue line) is within 1 km of the city of Firenze.

Aggregating data in SpatiaLite

Another thing that databases are really good at is aggregating data. For example, the following SQL query will count the number of towns per region:

```
SELECT Regions.Name, Regions.Geometry, count(*) as Count
FROM Regions
JOIN Towns
  ON Within(Towns.Geometry,Regions.Geometry)
GROUP BY Regions.Name
```

This can be used to create a new layer of regions that includes a Count attribute. This tells the number of towns in the region, as shown in this screenshot:

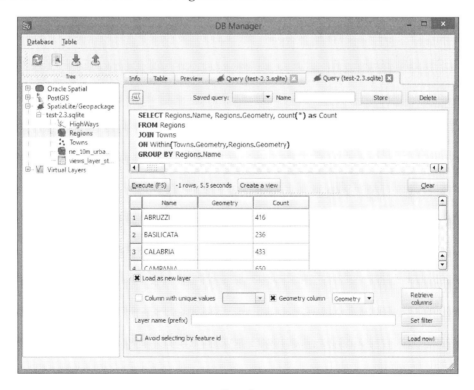

Although we have used SpatiaLite in this example, the tools and workflow presented here work just as well with PostGIS databases. It is worth noting, however, that SpatiaLite and PostGIS often use slightly different function names. Therefore, it is usually necessary to adjust the SQL queries accordingly.

Summary

In this chapter, we covered various raster and vector geoprocessing and analysis tools and how to apply them in common tasks. We saw how to use the Processing toolbox to run individual tools as well as the modeler to create complex geoprocessing models from multiple tools. Using the modeler, we can automate our workflows and increase our productivity, especially with respect to recurring tasks. Finally, we also had a quick look at how to leverage the power of spatial databases to perform spatial analysis.

In the following chapter, we will see how to bring all our knowledge together to create beautiful maps using advanced styles and print map composition features.

5
Creating Great Maps

In this chapter, we will cover the important features that enable us to create great maps. We will first go into advanced vector styling, building on what we covered in *Chapter 2*, *Viewing Spatial Data*. Then, you will learn how to label features by following examples for point labels as well as more advanced road labels with road shield graphics. We will also cover how to tweak labels manually. Then, you will get to know the print composer and how to use it to create printable maps and map books. Finally, we will explain how to create web maps directly in QGIS to present our results online.

 If you want to get an idea about what kind of map you can create using QGIS, visit the QGIS Map Showcase Flickr group at `https://www.flickr.com/groups/qgis/`, which is dedicated to maps created with QGIS without any further postprocessing.

Advanced vector styling

This section introduces more advanced vector styling features, building on the basics that we covered in *Chapter 2*, *Viewing Spatial Data*. We will cover how to create detailed custom visualizations using the following features:

- Graduated styles
- Categorized styles
- Rule-based styles
- Data-defined styles
- Heatmap styles
- 2.5D styles
- Layer effects

Creating a graduated style

Graduated styles are great for visualizing distributions of numerical values in choropleth or similar maps. The graduated renderer supports two methods:

- **Color**: This method changes the color of the feature according to the configured attribute

- **Size**: This method changes the symbol size for the feature according to the configured attribute (this option is only available for point and line layers)

In our sample data, there is a `climate.shp` file that contains locations and mean temperature values. We can visualize this data using a graduated style by simply selecting the **T_F_MEAN** value for the **Column** field and clicking on **Classify**. Using the **Color** method, as shown in the following screenshot, we can pick a **Color ramp** from the corresponding drop-down list. Additionally, we can reverse the order of the colors within the color ramp using the **Invert** option:

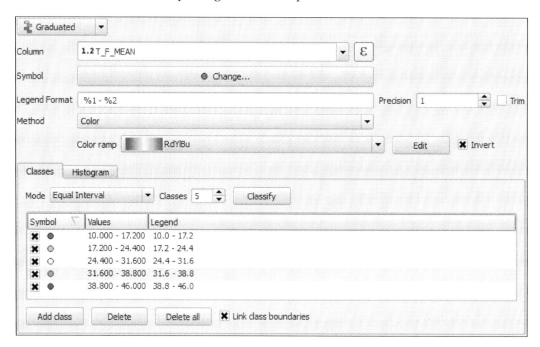

Graduated styles are available in different classification modes, as follows:

- **Equal Interval**: This mode creates classes by splitting at equal intervals between the maximum and minimum values found in the specified column.

- **Quantile (Equal Count)**: This mode creates classes so that each class contains an equal number of features.

- **Natural Breaks (Jenks)**: This mode uses the Jenks natural breaks algorithm to create classes by reducing variance within classes and maximizing variance between classes.

- **Standard Deviation**: This mode uses the column values' standard deviation to create classes.

- **Pretty Breaks**: This mode is the only classification that doesn't strictly create the specified number of classes. Instead, its main goal is to create class boundaries that are round numbers.

We can also manually edit the class values by double-clicking on the values in the list and changing the class bounds. A more convenient way to edit the classes is the **Histogram** view, as shown in the next screenshot. Switch to the **Histogram** tab and click on the **Load values** button in the bottom-right corner to enable the histogram. You can now edit the class bounds by moving the vertical lines with your mouse. You can also add new classes by adding a new vertical line, which you can do by clicking on empty space in the histogram:

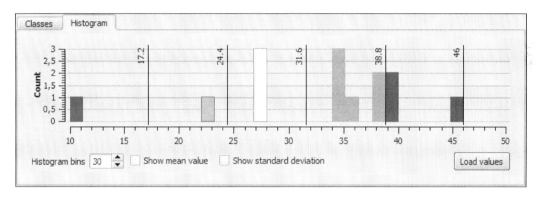

Besides the symbols that are drawn on the map, another important aspect of the styling is the **legend** that goes with it. To customize the legend, we can define **Legend Format** as well as the **Precision** (that is, the number of decimal places) that should be displayed. In the **Legend Format** string, %1 will be replaced by the lower limit of the class and %2 by the upper limit. You can change this string to suit your needs, for example, to this: from %1 to %2. If you activate the **Trim** option, excess trailing zeros will be removed as well.

When we use the **Size** method, as shown in the following screenshot, the dialog changes a little, and we can now configure the desired symbol sizes:

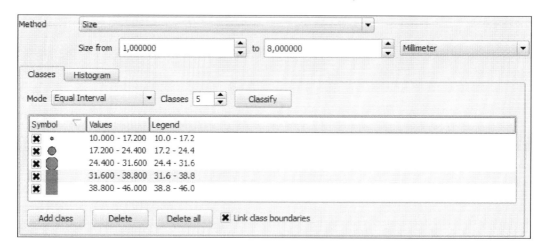

The next screenshot shows the results of using a **Graduated renderer** option with five classes using the **Equal Interval** classification mode. The left-hand side shows the results of the **Color** method (symbol color changes according to the T_F_MEAN value), while the right-hand side shows the results of the **Size** method (symbol size changes according to the T_F_MEAN value).

 Note the checkboxes besides each symbol. They can be used to selectively hide or show the features belonging to the corresponding class.

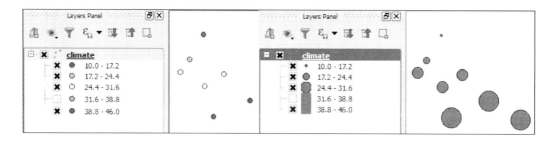

Creating and using color ramps

In the previous example, we used an existing color ramp to style our layer. Of course, we can also create our own color ramps. To create a new color ramp, we can scroll down the color ramp list to the **New color ramp...** entry. There are four different color ramp types, which we can chose from:

- **Gradient**: With this type, we can create color maps with two or more colors. The resulting color maps can be smooth gradients (using the **Continuous** type option) or distinct colors (using the **Discrete** type option), as shown in the following screenshot:

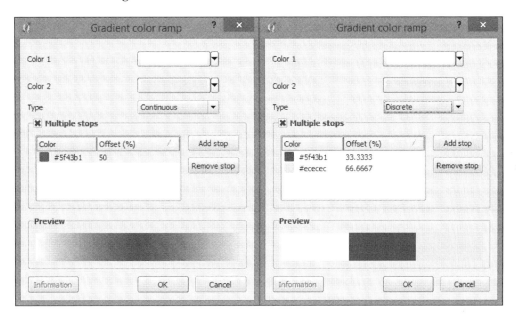

- **Random**: This type allows us to create a gradient with a certain number of random colors
- **ColorBrewer**: This type provides access to the **ColorBrewer** color schemes

- **cpt-city**: This type provides access to a wide variety of preconfigured color schemes, including schemes for typography and bathymetry, as shown in this screenshot:

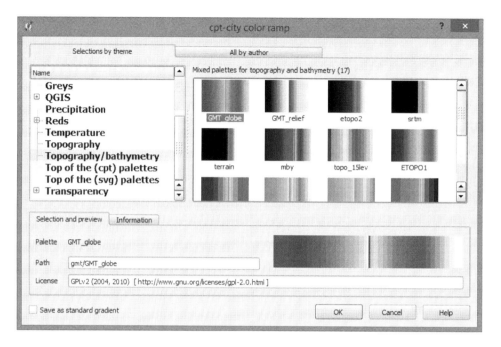

To manage all our color ramps and symbols, we can go to **Settings | Style Manager**. Here, we can add, delete, edit, export, or import color ramps and styles using the corresponding buttons on the right-hand side of the dialog, as shown in the following screenshot:

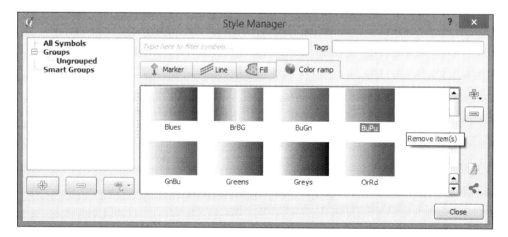

Using categorized styles for nominal data

Just as graduated styles are very useful for visualizing numeric values, categorized styles are great for text values or — more generally speaking — all kinds of values on a nominal scale. A good example for this kind of data can be found in the `trees.shp` file in our sample data. For each area, there is a **VEGDESC** value that describes the type of forest found there. Using a categorized style, we can easily generate a style with one symbol for every unique value in the **VEGDESC** column, as shown in the following screenshot. Once we click on **OK**, the style is applied to our trees layer in order to visualize the distribution of different tree types in the area:

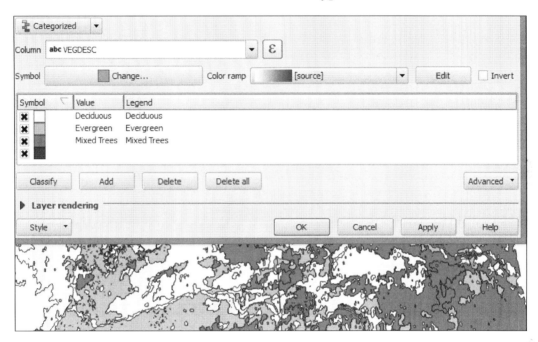

Of course, every symbol is editable and can be customized. Just double-click on the symbol preview to open the **Symbol** selector dialog, which allows you to select and combine different symbols.

Creating a rule-based style for road layers

With rule-based styles, we can create a layer style with a hierarchy of rules. Rules can take into account anything from attribute values to scale and geometry properties such as area or length. In this example, we will create a rule-based renderer for the `ne_10m_roads.shp` file from Natural Earth (you can download it from `http://www.naturalearthdata.com/downloads/10m-cultural-vectors/roads/`). As you can see here, our style will contain different road styles for major and secondary highways as well as scale-dependent styles:

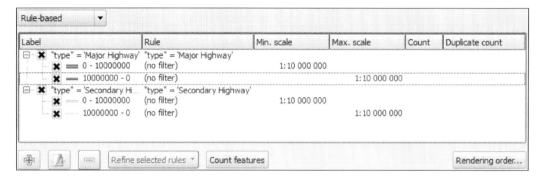

As you can see in the preceding screenshot, on the first level of rules, we distinguish between roads of **"type" = 'Major Highway'** and those of **"type" = 'Secondary Highway'**. The next level of rules handles **scale-dependence**. To add this second layer of rules, we can use the **Refine selected rules** button and select **Add scales to rule**. We simply input one or more scale values at which we want the rule to be split.

Note that there are no symbols specified on the first rule level. If we had symbols specified on the first level as well, the renderer would draw two symbols over each other. While this can be useful in certain cases, we don't want this effect right now. Symbols can be deactivated in **Rule properties**, which is accessible by double-clicking on the rule or clicking on the edit button below the rule's tree view (the button between the plus and minus buttons).

In the following screenshot, we can see the rule-based renderer and the scale rules in action. While the left-hand side shows wider white roads with grey outlines for secondary highways, the right-hand side shows the simpler symbology with thin grey lines:

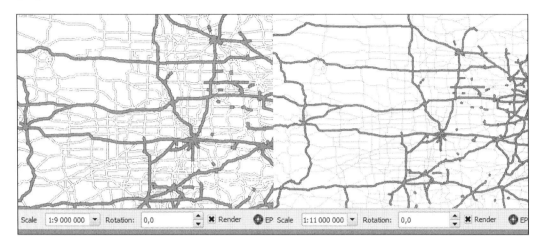

You can download the symbols used in this style by going to **Settings | Style Manager**, clicking on the sharing button in the bottom-right corner of the dialog, and selecting **Import**. The URL is `https://raw.githubusercontent.com/anitagraser/QGIS-resources/master/qgis1.8/symbols/osm_symbols.xml`. Paste the URL in the **Location** textbox, click on **Fetch Symbols**, then click on **Select all**, and finally click on **Import**. The dialog will look like what is shown in the following screenshot:

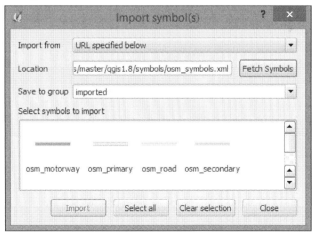

Creating data-defined symbology

In previous examples, we created categories or rules to define how features are drawn on a map. An alternative approach is to use values from the layer attribute table to define the styling. This can be achieved using a QGIS feature called **Data defined override**. These overrides can be configured using the corresponding buttons next to each symbol property, as described in the following example.

In this example, we will again use the `ne_10m_roads.shp` file from Natural Earth. The next screenshot shows a configuration that creates a style where the line's **Pen width** depends on the feature's `scalerank` and the line **Color** depends on the `toll` attribute. To set a data-defined override for a symbol property, you need to click on the corresponding button, which is located right next to the property, and choose **Edit**. The following two expressions are used:

- `CASE WHEN toll = 1 THEN 'red' ELSE 'lightgray' END`: This expression evaluates the `toll` value. If it is `1`, the line is drawn in red; otherwise, it is drawn in gray.

- `2.5 / scalerank`: This expression computes **Pen width**. Since a low scale rank should be represented by a wider line, we use a division operation instead of multiplication.

When data-defined overrides are active, the corresponding buttons are highlighted in yellow with an ε sign on them, as shown in the following screenshot:

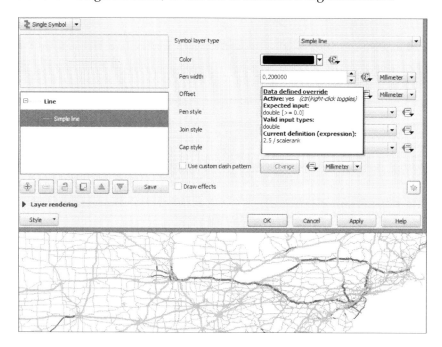

In this example, you have seen that you can specify colors using **color names** such as `'red'`, `'gold'`, and `'deepskyblue'`. Another especially useful group of functions for data-defined styles is the **Color** functions. There are functions for the following **color models**:

- **RGB**: `color_rgb(red, green, blue)`
- **HSL**: `color_hsl(hue, saturation, lightness)`
- **HSV**: `color_hsv(hue, saturation, value)`
- **CMYK**: `color_cmyk(cyan, magenta, yellow, black)`

There are also functions for accessing the color ramps. Here are two examples of how to use these functions:

- `ramp_color('Reds', T_F_MEAN / 46)`: This expression returns a color from the `Reds` color ramp depending on the `T_F_MEAN` value. Since the second parameter has to be a value between `0` and `1`, we divide the `T_F_MEAN` value by the maximum value, `46`.

Since users can add new color ramps or change existing ones, the color ramps can vary between different QGIS installations. Therefore, the `ramp_color` function may return different results if the style or project file is used on a different computer.

- `color_rgba(0, 0, 180, scale_linear(T_F_JUL - T_F_JAN, 20, 70, 0, 255))`: This expression computes the color depending on the difference between the July and January temperatures, `T_F_JUL - T_F_JAN`. The difference value is transformed into a value between `0` and `255` by the `scale_linear` function according to the following rule: any value up to `20` will be translated to `0`, any value of `70` and above will be translated to `255`, and anything in between will be interpolated linearly. Bigger difference values result in darker colors because of the higher alpha parameter value.

The alpha component in RGBA, HSLA, HSVA, and CMYKA controls the transparency of the color. It can take on an integer value from `0` (completely transparent) to `255` (opaque).

Creating a dynamic heatmap style

In *Chapter 4*, *Spatial Analysis*, you learned how to create a heatmap raster. However, there is a faster, more convenient way to achieve this look if you want a heatmap only for displaying purposes (and not for further spatial analysis)—the **Heatmap** renderer option.

The following screenshot shows a **Heatmap** renderer set up for our populated places dataset, popp.shp. We can specify a color ramp that will be applied to the resulting heatmap values between 0 and the defined **Maximum value**. If **Maximum value** is set to **Automatic**, QGIS automatically computes the highest value in the heatmap. As in the previously discussed heatmap tool, we can define point weights as well as the kernel **Radius** (for an explanation of this term, check out *Creating a heatmap from points* in *Chapter 4*, *Spatial Analysis*). The final **Rendering quality** option controls the quality of the rendered output with coarse, big raster cells for the **Fastest** option and a fine-grained look when set to **Best**:

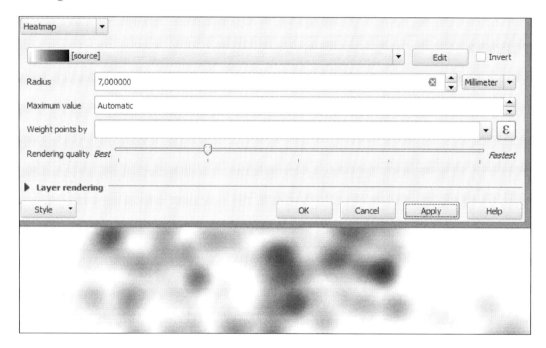

Creating a 2.5D style

If you want to create a pseudo-3D look, for example, to style building blocks or to create a thematic map, try the 2.5D renderer. The next screenshot shows the current configuration options that include controls for the feature's **Height** (in layer units), the viewing **Angle**, and colors. Since this renderer is still being improved at the time of writing this book, you might find additional options in this dialog when you see it for yourself.

Once you have configured the 2.5D renderer to your liking, you can switch to another renderer to, for example, create classified or graduated versions of symbols.

Adding live layer effects

With **layer effects**, we can change the way our symbols look even further. Effects can be added by enabling the **Draw effects** checkbox at the bottom of the symbol dialog, as shown in the following screenshot. To configure the effects, click on the Star button in the bottom-right corner of the dialog. The **Effect Properties** dialog offers access to a wide range of **Effect types**:

- **Blur**: This effect creates a blurred, fuzzy version of the symbol.

- **Colorise**: This effect changes the color of the symbol.

- **Source**: This is the original unchanged symbol.

- **Drop Shadow**: This effect creates a shadow.

- **Inner Glow**: This effect creates a glow-like gradient that extends inwards, starting from the symbol border.

- **Inner Shadow**: This effect creates a shadow that is restricted to the inside of the symbol.

- **Outer Glow**: This effect creates a glow that radiates from the symbol outwards.

- **Transform**: This effect can be used to transform the symbol. The available transformations include reflect, shear, scale, rotate, and translate:

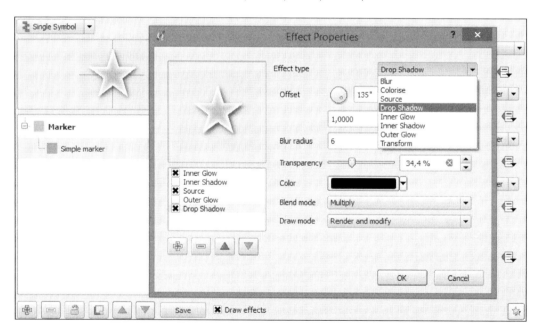

As you can see in the previous screenshot, we can combine multiple layer effects and they are organized in effect layers in the list in the bottom-left corner of the **Effect Properties** dialog.

Working with different styles

When we create elaborate styles, we might want to save them so that we can reuse them in other projects or share them with other users. To save a style, click on the **Style** button in the bottom-left corner of the style dialog and go to **Save Style | QGIS Layer Style File...**, as shown in the following screenshot. This will create a .qml file, which you can save anywhere, copy, and share with others. Similarly, to use the .qml file, click on the **Style** button and select **Load Style**:

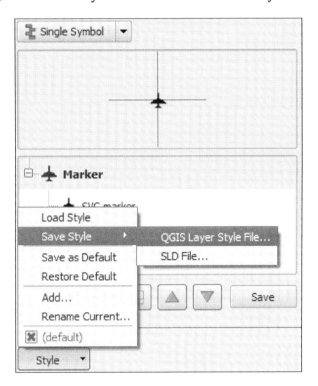

We can also save multiple different styles for one layer. For example, for our airports layer, we might want one style that displays airports using plane symbols and another style that renders a heatmap. To achieve this, we can do the following:

1. Configure the plane style.

2. Click on the **Style** button and select **Add** to add the current style to the list of styles for this layer.

3. In the pop-up dialog, enter a name for the new style, for example, `planes`.

4. Add another style by clicking on **Style** and **Add** and call it `heatmap`.

5. Now, you can change the renderer to **Heatmap** and configure it. Click on the **Apply** button when ready.

6. In the **Style** button menu, you can now see both styles, as shown in the next screenshot. Changing from one style to the other is now as simple as selecting one of the two entries from the list at the bottom of this menu:

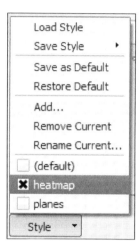

Finally, we can also access these layer styles through the layer context menu **Styles** entry in the **Layers Panel**, as shown in the following screenshot. This context menu also provides a way to copy and paste styles between layers using the **Copy Style** and **Paste Style** entries, respectively. Furthermore, this context menu provides a shortcut to quickly change the symbol color using a color wheel or by picking a color from the **Recent colors** section:

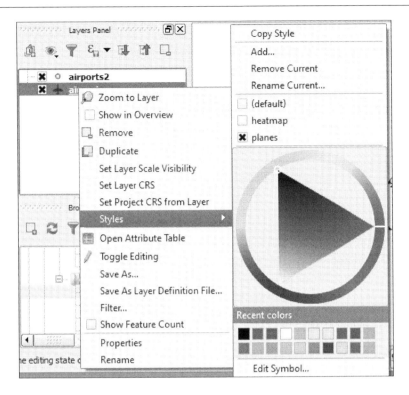

Labeling

We can activate labeling by going to **Layer Properties | Labels**, selecting **Show labels for this layer**, and selecting the attribute field that we want to **Label with**. This is all we need to do to display labels with default settings. While default labels are great for a quick preview, we will usually want to customize labels if we create visualizations for reports or standalone maps.

Using **Expressions** (the button that is right beside the attribute drop-down list), we can format the label text to suit our needs. For example, the **NAME** field in our sample `airports.shp` file contains text in uppercase. To display the airport names in mixed case instead, we can set the `title(NAME)` expression, which will reformat the name text in title case. We can also use multiple fields to create a label, for example, combining the name and elevation in brackets using the concatenation operator (| |), as follows:

```
title(NAME) || ' (' || "ELEV" || ')'
```

Note the use of simple quotation marks around text, such as ' (', and double quotation marks around field names, such as "ELEV". The dialog will look like what is shown in this screenshot:

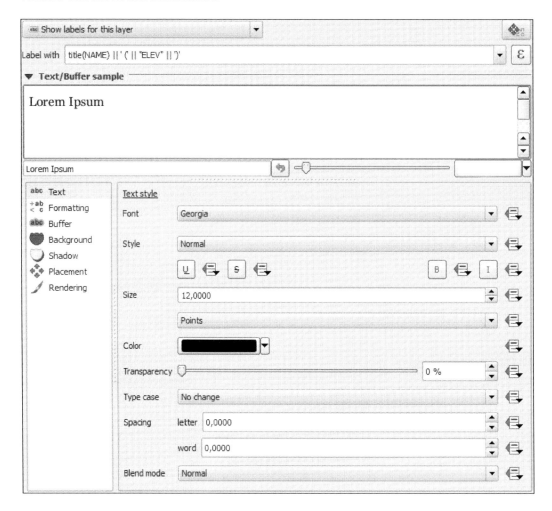

The big preview area at the top of the dialog, titled **Text/Buffer sample**, shows a preview of the current settings. The background color can be adjusted to test readability on different backgrounds. Under the preview area, we find the different label settings, which will be described in detail in the following sections.

Customizing label text styles

In the **Text** section (shown in the previous screenshot), we can configure the text style. Besides changing **Font**, **Style**, **Size**, **Color**, and **Transparency**, we can also modify the **Spacing** between **letters** and **words**, as well as **Blend mode**, which works like the layer blending mode that we covered in *Chapter 2*, *Viewing Spatial Data*.

Note the column of buttons on the right-hand side of every setting. Clicking on these buttons allows us to create data-defined overrides, similar to those that we discussed at the beginning of the chapter when we talked about advanced vector styling. These data-defined overrides can be used, for example, to define different label colors or change the label size depending on an individual feature's attribute value or an expression.

Controlling label formatting

In the **Formatting** section, which is shown in the following screenshot, we can enable **multiline labels** by specifying a **Wrap on character**. Additionally, we can control **Line height** and **Alignment**. Besides the typical alignment options, the QGIS labeling engine also provides a **Follow label placement** option, which ensures that multiline labels are aligned towards the same side as the symbol the label belongs to:

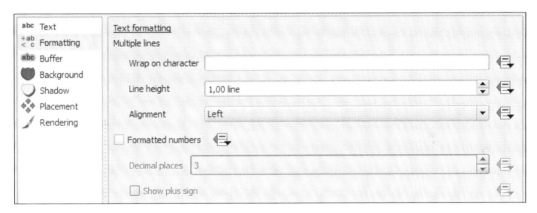

Finally, the **Formatted numbers** option offers a shortcut to format numerical values to a certain number of **Decimal places**.

An alternative to wrapping text on a certain character is the `wordwrap` function, available in expressions. It wraps the input string to a certain maximum or minimum number of characters. The following screenshot shows an example of wrapping a longer piece of text to a maximum of 22 characters per line:

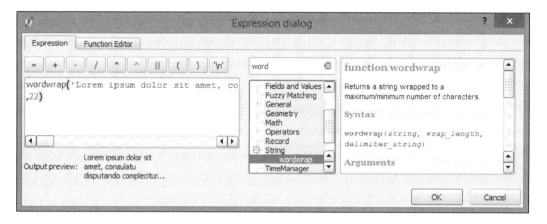

Configuring label buffers, background, and shadows

In the **Buffer** section, we can adjust the buffer **Size**, **Color**, and **Transparency**, as well as **Pen join style** and **Blend mode**. With transparency and blending, we can improve label readability without blocking out the underlying map too much, as shown in the following screenshot.

In the **Background** section, we can add a background shape in the form of a rectangle, square, circle, ellipsoid, or SVG. SVG backgrounds are great for creating effects such as **highway shields**, which we will discuss shortly.

Similarly, in the **Shadow** section, we can add a shadow to our labels. We can control everything from shadow direction to **Color**, **Blur radius**, **Scale**, and **Transparency**.

Controlling label placement

In the **Placement** section, we can configure which rules should be used to determine where the labels are placed. The available automatic label placement options depend on the layer geometry type.

Configuring point labels

For *point layers*, we can choose from the following:

- The flexible **Around point** option tries to find the best position for labels by distributing them around the points without overlaps. As you can see in the following screenshot, some labels are put in the top-right corner of their point symbol while others appear at different positions on the left (for example, **Anchorage Intl (129)**) or right (for example, **Big Lake (135)**) side.

- The **Offset from point** option forces all labels to a certain position; for example, all labels can be placed above their point symbol.

The following screenshot shows airport labels with a 50 percent transparent **Buffer** and **Drop Shadow**, placed using **Around point**. The **Label distance** is 1 mm.

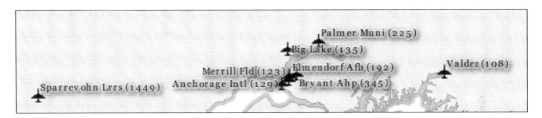

Configuring line labels

For *line layers*, we can choose from the following placement options:

- **Parallel** for straight labels that are rotated according to the line orientation
- **Curved** for labels that follow the shape of the line
- **Horizontal** for labels that keep a horizontal orientation, regardless of the line orientation

For further fine-tuning, we can define whether the label should be placed **Above line**, **On line**, or **Below line**, and how far above or below it should be placed using **Label distance**.

Configuring polygon labels

For *polygon layers*, the placement options are as follows:

- **Offset from centroid** uses the polygon centroid as an anchor and works like **Offset from point** for point layers
- **Around centroid** works in a manner similar to **Around point**

- **Horizontal** places a horizontal label somewhere inside the polygon, independent of the centroid

- **Free** fits a freely rotated label inside the polygon

- **Using perimeter** places the label on the polygon's outline

The following screenshot shows lake labels (`lakes.shp`) using the **Multiple lines** feature wrapping on the empty space character, **Center Alignment**, a **Letter spacing** of 2, and positioning using the **Free** option:

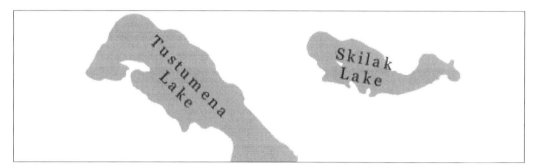

Placing labels manually

Besides automatic label placement, we also have the option to use **data-defined placement** to position labels exactly where we want them to be. In the labeling toolbar, we find tools for moving and rotating labels by hand. They are active and available only for layers that have set up data-defined placement for at least *X* and *Y* coordinates:

1. To start using the tools, we can simply add three new columns, `label_x`, `label_y`, and `label_rot` to, for example, the `airports.shp` file. We don't have to enter any values in the attribute table right now. The labeling engine will check for values, and if it finds the attribute fields empty, it will simply place the labels automatically.

2. Then, we can specify these columns in the label **Placement** section. Configure the data-defined overrides by clicking on the buttons beside **Coordinate X**, **Coordinate Y**, and **Rotation**, as shown in the following screenshot:

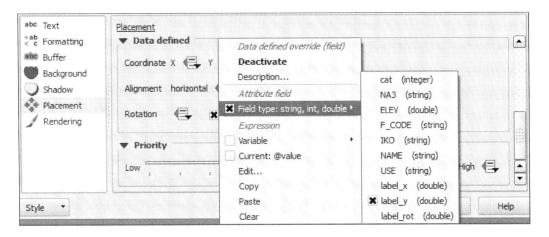

3. By specifying data-defined placement, the labeling toolbar's tools are now available (note that the editing mode has to be turned on), and we can use the **Move label** and **Rotate label** tools to manipulate the labels on the map. The changes are written back to the attribute table.

4. Try moving some labels, especially where they are placed closely together, and watch how the automatically placed labels adapt to your changes.

Controlling label rendering

In the **Rendering** section, we can define **Scale-based visibility** limits to display labels only at certain scales and **Pixel size-based visibility** to hide labels for small features. Here, we can also tell the labeling engine to **Show all labels for this layer (including colliding labels)**, which are normally hidden by default.

The following example shows labels with **road shields**. You can download a blank road shield SVG from `http://upload.wikimedia.org/wikipedia/commons/c/c3/ Blank_shield.svg`. Note how only `Interstates` are labeled. This can be achieved using the **Data defined Show label** setting in the **Rendering** section with the following expression:

```
"level" = 'Interstate'
```

The labels are positioned using the **Horizontal** option (in the **Placement** section). Additionally, **Merge connected lines to avoid duplicate labels** and **Suppress labeling of features smaller than** are activated; for example, 5 mm helps avoid clutter by not labeling pieces of road that are shorter than 5 mm in the current scale.

To set up the road shield, go to the **Background** section and select the blank shield SVG from the folder you downloaded it in. To make sure that the label fits nicely inside the shield, we additionally specify the **Size type** field as a buffer with a **Size** of 1 mm. This makes the shield a little bigger than the label it contains.

If you click on **Apply** now, you will notice that the labels are not centered perfectly inside the shields. To fix this, we apply a small **Offset** in the **Y** direction to the shield position, as shown in the following screenshot. Additionally, it is recommended that you deactivate any label buffers as they tend to block out parts of the shield, and we don't need them anyway.

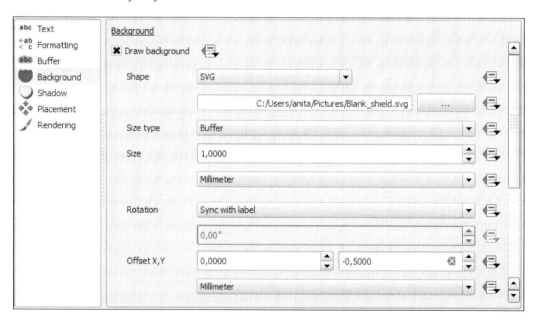

Designing print maps

In QGIS, **print maps** are designed in the print composer. A QGIS project can contain multiple composers, so it makes sense to pick descriptive names. Composers are saved automatically whenever we save the project. To see a list of all the compositions available in a project, go to **Project | Composer Manager**.

We can open a new composer by going to **Project | New Print Composer** or using *Ctrl + P*. The composer window consists of the following:

* A preview area for the map composition displaying a blank page when a new composer is created

* Panels for configuring **Composition**, **Item properties**, and **Atlas generation**, as well as a **Command history** panel for quick undo and redo actions

* Toolbars to manage, save, and export compositions; navigate in the preview area; as well as add and arrange different composer items

Once you have designed your print map the way you want it, you can save the template to a **composer template** .qpt file by going to **Composer | Save as template** and reuse it in other projects by going to **Composer | Add Items from Template**.

Creating a basic map

In this example, we will create a basic map with a scalebar, a north arrow, some explanatory text, and a legend.

When we start the print composer, we first see the **Composition** panel on the right-hand side. This panel gives us access to paper options such as size, orientation, and number of pages. It is also the place to configure snapping behavior and output resolution.

First, we add a map item to the paper using the **Add new map** button, or by going to **Layout | Add Map** and drawing the map rectangle on the paper. Click on the paper, keep the mouse button pressed down, and drag the rectangle open. We can move and resize the map using the mouse and the **Select/Move item** tools. Alternatively, it is possible to configure all the map settings in the **Item properties** panel.

The **Item properties** panel's content depends on the currently selected composition item. If a map item is selected, we can adjust the map's **Scale** and **Extents** as well as the **Position and size** tool of the map item itself. At a **Scale** of 10,000,000 (with the CRS set to EPSG:2964), we can more or less fit a map of Alaska on an A4-size paper, as shown in the following screenshot. To move the area that is displayed within the map item and change the map scale, we can use the **Move item content** tool.

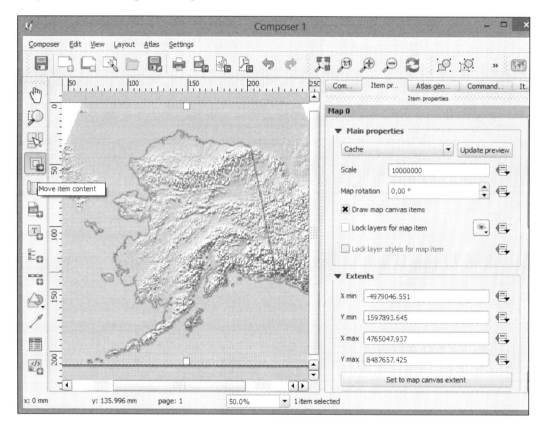

Adding a scalebar

After the map looks like what we want it to, we can add a scalebar using the **Add new scalebar** button or by going to **Layout | Add Scalebar** and clicking on the map. The **Item properties** panel now displays the scalebar's properties, which are similar to what you can see in the next screenshot. Since we can add multiple map items to one composition, it is important to specify which map the scale belongs to. The second main property is the scalebar **style**, which allows us to choose between different scalebar types, or a **Numeric** type for a simple textual representation, such as 1:10,000,000. Using the **Units** properties, we can convert the map units in feet or meters to something more manageable, such as miles or kilometers. The **Segments** properties control the number of segments and the size of a single segment in the scalebar. Further, the properties control the scalebar's color, font, background, and so on.

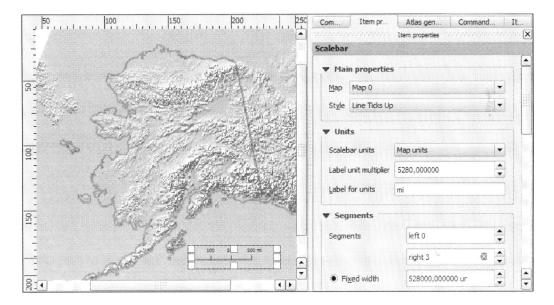

Adding a North arrow image

North arrows can be added to a composition using the **Add Image** button or by going to **Layout** | **Add image** and clicking on the paper. To use one of the SVGs that are part of the QGIS installation, open the **Search directories** section in the **Item properties** panel. It might take a while for QGIS to load the previews of the images in the SVG folder. You can pick a North arrow from the list of images or select your own image by clicking on the button next to the **Image source** input. More map decorations, such as arrows or rectangle, triangle, and ellipse shapes can be added using the appropriate toolbar buttons: **Add Arrow**, **Add Rectangle**, and so on.

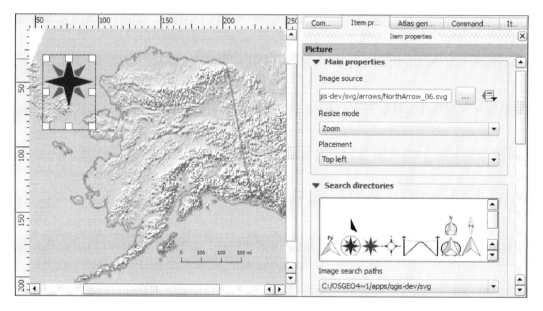

Adding a legend

Legends are another vital map element. We can use the **Add new legend** button or go to **Layout** | **Add legend** to add a default legend with entries for all currently visible map layers. Legend entries can be reorganized (sorted or added to groups), edited, and removed from the legend items' properties. Using the **Wrap text on** option, we can split long labels on multiple rows. The following screenshot shows the context menu that allows us to change the style (**Hidden**, **Group**, or **Subgroup**) of an entry. The corresponding font, size, and color are configurable in the **Fonts** section.

Additionally, the legend in this example is divided into three **Columns**, as you can see in the bottom-right section of the following screenshot. By default, QGIS tries to keep all entries of one layer in a single column, but we can override this behavior by enabling **Split layers**.

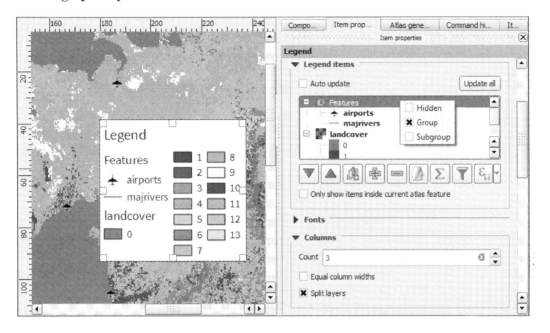

Adding explanatory text to the map

To add text to the map, we can use the **Add new label** button or go to **Layout | Add label**. Simple labels display all text using the same font. By enabling **Render as HTML**, we can create more elaborate labels with headers, lists, different colors, and highlights in bold or italics using normal HTML notation. Here is an example:

```
<h1>Alaska</h1>
<p>The name <i>"Alaska"</i> means "the mainland".</p>
<ul><li>one list entry</li><li>another entry</li></ul>
<p style="font-size:70%;">[% format_date( $now ,'yyyy-mm-dd')%]</p>
```

Labels can also contain expressions such as these:

- `[% $now %]`: This expression inserts the current timestamp, which can be formatted using the `format_date` function, as shown in the following screenshot

- `[% $page %] of [% $numpages %]`: This expression can be used to insert page numbers in compositions with multiple pages

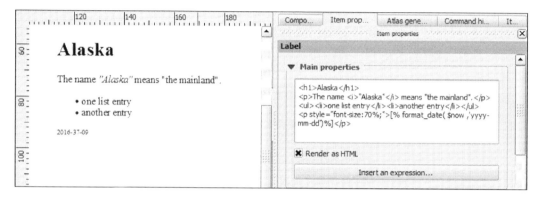

Adding map grids and frames

Other common features of maps are **grids** and **frames**. Every map item can have one or more grids. Click on the **+** button in the **Grids** section to add a grid. The **Interval** and **Offset** values have to be specified in map units. We can choose between the following **Grid types**:

- A normal **Solid** grid with customizable lines

- **Crosses** at specified intervals with customizable styles

- **Customizable Markers** at specified intervals

- **Frame and annotation only** will hide the grid while still displaying the frame and coordinate annotations

For **Grid frame**, we can select from the following **Frame styles**:

- **Zebra**, with customizable line and fill colors, as shown in the following screenshot

- **Interior ticks**, **Exterior ticks**, or **Interior and exterior ticks** for tick marks pointing inside the map, outside it, or in both directions

- **Line border** for a simple line frame

Using **Draw coordinates**, we can label the grid with the corresponding coordinates. The labels can be aligned horizontally or vertically and placed inside or outside the frame, as shown here:

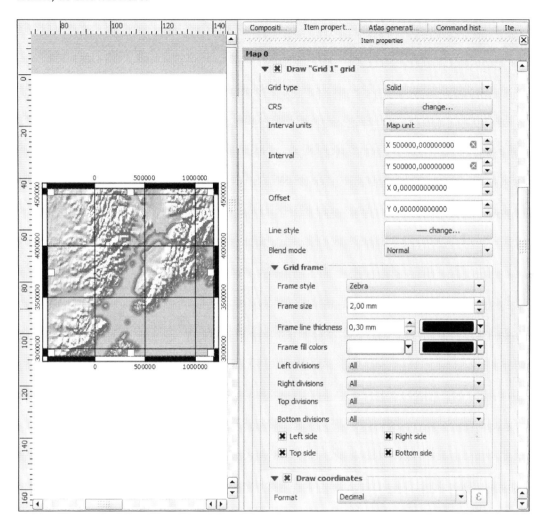

Creating overview maps

Maps that show an area close up are often accompanied by a second map that tells the reader where the area is located in a larger context. To create such an **overview map**, we add a second map item and an overview by clicking on the + button in the **Overviews** section. By setting the **Map frame**, we can define which detail map's extent should be highlighted. By clicking on the + button again, we can add more map frames to the overview map. The following screenshot shows an example with two detail maps both of which are added to an overview map. To distinguish between the two maps, the overview highlights are color-coded (by changing the overview **Frame style**) to match the colors of the frames of the detail maps.

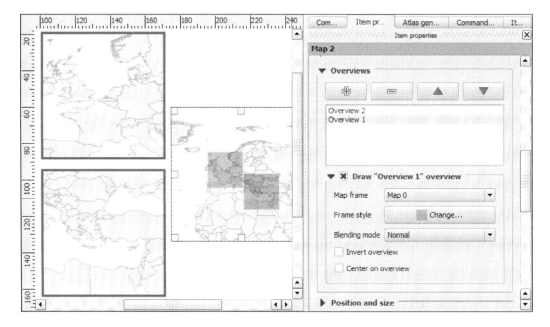

 Every map item in a composition can display a different combination of layers. Generally, map items in a composer are synced with the map in the main QGIS window. So, if we turn a layer off in the main window, it is removed from the print composer map as well. However, we can stop this automatic synchronization by enabling **Lock layers** for a map item in the map item's properties.

Adding more details with attribute tables and HTML frames

To insert additional details into the map, the composer also offers the possibility of adding an **attribute table** to the composition using the **Add attribute table** button or by going to **Layout | Add attribute table**. By enabling **Show only features visible within a map**, we can filter the table and display only the relevant results. Additional filter expressions can be set using the **Filter with** option. Sorting (by name for example, as shown in the following screenshot) and renaming of columns is possible via the **Attributes** button. To customize the header row with bold and centered text, go to the **Fonts and text styling** section and change the **Table heading** settings.

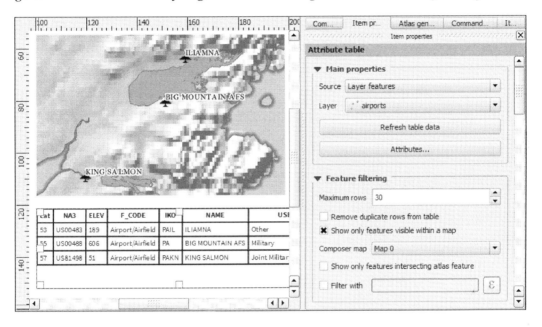

Even more advanced content can be added using the **Add html frame** button. We can point the item's URL reference to any HTML page on our local machines or online, and the content (text and images as displayed in a web browser) will be displayed on the composer page.

Creating a map series using the Atlas feature

With the print composer's Atlas feature, we can create a series of maps using one print composition. The tool will create one output (which can be image files, PDFs, or multiple pages in one PDF) for every feature in the so-called **Coverage layer**.

Atlas can control and update multiple map items within one composition. To enable Atlas for a map item, we have to enable the **Controlled by atlas** option in the **Item properties** of the map item. When we use the **Fixed scale** option in the **Controlled by atlas** section, all maps will be rendered using the same scale. If we need a more flexible output, we can switch to the **Margin around feature** option instead, which zooms to every **Coverage layer** feature and renders it in addition to the specified margin surrounding area.

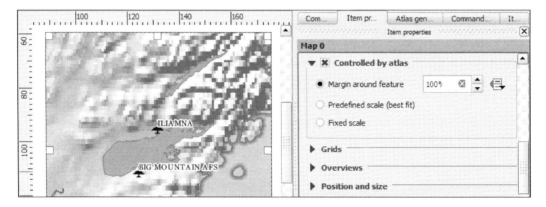

To finish the configuration, we switch to the **Atlas generation** panel. As mentioned before, Atlas will create one map for every feature in the layer configured in the **Coverage layer** dropdown. Features in the coverage layer can be displayed like regular features or hidden by enabling **Hidden coverage layer**. Adding an expression to the **Feature filtering** option or enabling the **Sort by** option makes it possible to further fine-tune the results. The **Output** field can be one image or PDF for each coverage layer feature, or you can create a multipage PDF by enabling **Single file export when possible** before going to **Composer | Export as PDF**.

Once these configurations are finished, we can preview the map series by enabling the **Preview Atlas** button, which you can see in the top-left corner of the following screenshot. The arrow buttons next to the preview button are used to navigate between the Atlas maps.

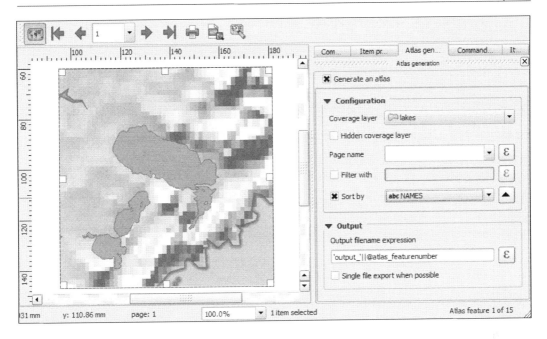

Presenting your maps online

Besides print maps, web maps are another popular way of publishing maps. In this section, we will use different QGIS plugins to create different types of web map.

Exporting a web map

To create web maps from within QGIS, we can use the **qgis2web** plugin, which we have to install using the **Plugin Manager**. Once it is installed, go to **Web | qgis2web | Create web map** to start it. **qgis2web** supports the two most popular open source **web mapping libraries**: **OpenLayers 3**, and **Leaflet**.

The following screenshot shows an example of our airports dataset. In this example, we are using the **Leaflet** library (as configured in the bottom-left corner of the following screenshot) because at the time of writing this book, only **Leaflet** supports SVG markers:

1. In the top-left corner, you can configure which layers from your project should be displayed on the web map, as well as the **Info popup content**, which is displayed when the user clicks on or hovers over a feature (depending on the **Show popups on hover** setting).

2. In the bottom-right corner, you can pick a background map for your web map. Pick one and click on the **Update preview** button to see the result.

3. In the bottom-left corner, you can further configure the web map. All available settings are documented in the **Help** tab, so the content is not reproduced here. Again, don't forget to click on the **Update preview** button when you make changes.

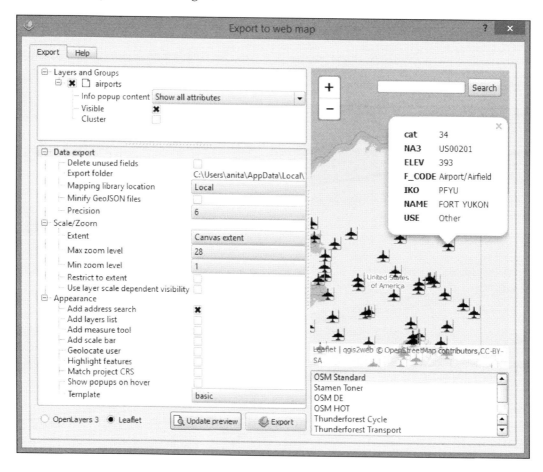

When you are happy with the configuration, click on the **Export** button. This will save the web map at the location specified as the **Export folder** and open the resulting web map in your web browser. You can copy the contents in the **Export folder** to a web server to publish the map.

Creating map tiles

Another popular way to share maps on the Web is **map tiles**. These are basically just collections of images. These image tiles are typically 256 × 256 pixels and are placed side by side in order to create an illusion of a very large, seamless map image. Each tile has a z coordinate that describes its zoom level and x and y coordinates that describe its position within a square grid for that zoom level. On zoom level 0 ($z0$), the whole world fits in one tile. From there on, each consecutive zoom level is related to the previous one by a power of 4. This means $z0$ contains 1 tile, $z1$ contains 4 tiles, and $z2$ contains 16 tiles, and so on.

In QGIS, we can use the **QTiles** plugin, which has to be installed using the **Plugin Manager**, to create map tiles for our project. Once it is installed, you can go to **Plugins | QTiles** to start it. The following screenshot shows the plugin dialog where we can configure the **Output** location, the **Extent** of the map that we want to export as tiles, as well as the **Zoom** levels we want to create tiles for.

When you click on **OK**, the plugin will create a `.zip` file containing all tiles. Using map tiles in web mapping libraries is out of the scope of this book. Please refer to the documentation of your web mapping library for instructions on how to embed the tiles. If you are using Leaflet, for example, you can refer to `https://switch2osm.org/using-tiles/getting-started-with-leaflet` for detailed instructions.

Exporting a 3D web map

To create stunning **3D web maps**, we need the **Qgis2threejs** plugin, which we can install using the **Plugin Manager**.

For example, we can use our `srtm_05_01.tif` elevation dataset to create a 3D view of that part of Alaska. The following screenshot shows the configuration of **DEM Layer** in the **Qgis2threejs** dialog. By selecting **Display type** as **Map canvas image**, we furthermore define that the current map image (which is shown on the right-hand side of the dialog) will be draped over the 3D surface:

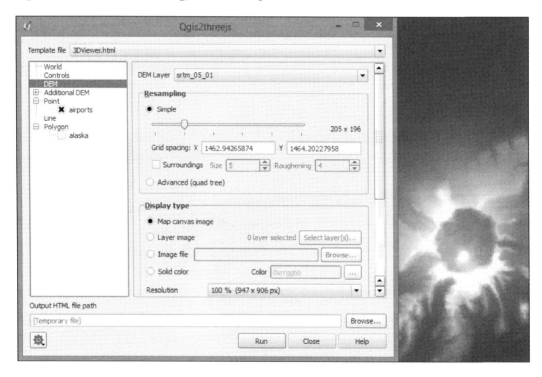

Besides creating a 3D surface, this plugin can also label features. For example, we can add our airports and label them with their names, as shown in the next screenshot. By setting **Label height** to **Height from point**, we let the plugin determine automatically where to place the label, but of course, you can manually override this by changing to **Fixed value** or one of the feature attributes.

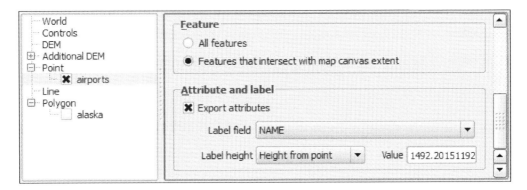

If you click on **Run** now, the plugin will create the export and open the 3D map in your web browser. On the first try, it is quite likely that the surface looks too flat. Luckily, this can be changed easily by adjusting the **Vertical exaggeration** setting in the **World** section of the plugin configuration. The following example was created with a **Vertical exaggeration** of 10:

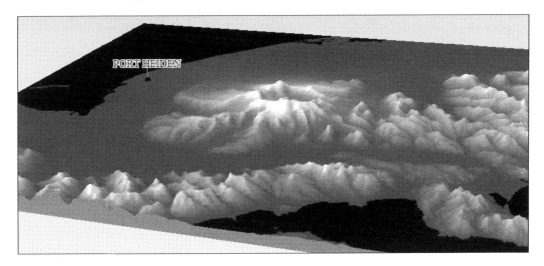

Qgis2threejs exports all files to the location specified in the **Output HTML file path**. You can copy the contents in that folder on a web server to publish the map.

Summary

In this chapter, we took a closer look at how we can create more complex maps using advanced vector layer styles, such as categorized or rule-based styles. We also covered the automatic and manual feature labeling options available in QGIS. This chapter also showed you how to create printable maps using the print composer and introduced the Atlas functionality for creating map books. Finally, we created web maps, which we can publish online.

Congratulations! In the chapters so far, you have learned how to install and use QGIS to create, edit, and analyze spatial data and how to present it in an effective manner. In the following and final chapter, we will take a look at expanding QGIS functionality using Python.

6

Extending QGIS with Python

This chapter is an introduction to scripting QGIS with Python. Of course, a full-blown Python tutorial would be out of scope for this book. The examples here therefore assume a minimum proficiency of working with Python. Python is a very accessible programming language even if you are just getting started, and it has gained a lot of popularity in both the open source and proprietary GIS world, for example, ESRI's **ArcPy** or **PyQGIS**. QGIS currently supports **Python 2.7**, but there are plans to support Python 3 in the upcoming **QGIS 3.x** series. We will start with an introduction to actions and then move on to the QGIS Python Console, before we go into more advanced development of custom tools for the *Processing Toolbox* and an explanation of how to create our own plugins.

Adding functionality using actions

Actions are a convenient way of adding custom functionality to QGIS. Actions are created for specific layers, for example, our populated places dataset, popp.shp. Therefore, to create actions, we go to **Layer Properties | Actions**. There are different types of actions, such as the following:

- **Generic actions** start external processes; for example, you run command-line applications such as ogr2ogr

  [ogr2ogr is a command-line tool that can be used to convert file formats and, at the same time, perform operations such as spatial or attribute selections and reprojecting.]

- **Python actions** execute Python scripts

- **Open actions** open a file using your computer's configured default application, that is, your PDF viewing application for `.pdf` files or your browser for websites

- Operating system (**Mac**, **Windows**, and **Unix**) actions work like generic actions but are restricted to the respective operating system

Configuring your first Python action

Click on the **Add default actions** button on the right-hand side of the dialog to add some example actions to your popp layer. This is really handy to get started with actions. For example, the Python action called **Selected field's value** will display the specified attribute's value when we use the action tool. All that we need to do before we can give this action a try is update it so that it accesses a valid attribute of our layer. For example, we can make it display the popp layer's TYPE attribute value in a message box, as shown in the next screenshot:

1. Select the **Selected field's value** action in **Action list**.

2. Edit the **Action** code at the bottom of the dialog. You can manually enter the attribute name or select it from the drop-down list and click on **Insert field**.

3. To save the changes, click on **Update selected action**:

To use this action, close the **Layer Properties** dialog and click on the drop-down arrow next to the **Run Feature Action** button. This will expand the list of available layer actions, as shown in the following screenshot:

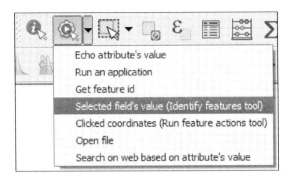

Click on the **Selected field's value** entry and then click on a layer feature. This will open a pop-up dialog in which the action will output the feature's TYPE value. Of course, we can also make this action output more information, for example, by extending it to this:

```
QtGui.QMessageBox.information(None, "Current field's value",
"Type: [% "TYPE" %] \n[% "F_CODEDESC" %]")
```

This will display the TYPE value on the first line and the F_CODEDESC value on the second line.

Opening files using actions

To open files directly from within QGIS, we use the **Open** actions. If you added the default actions in the previous exercise, your layer will already have an **Open file** action. The action is as simple as `[% "PATH" %]` for opening the file path specified in the layer's path attribute. Since none of our sample datasets contain a path attribute, we'll add one now to test this feature. Check out *Chapter 3, Data Creation and Editing,* if you need to know the details of how to add a new attribute. For example, the paths added in the following screenshot will open the default image viewer and PDF viewer application, respectively:

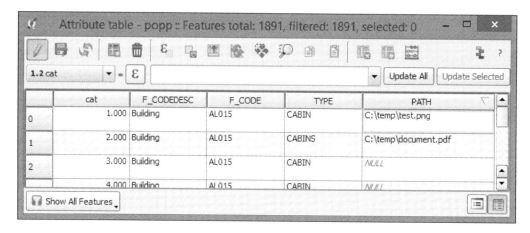

While the previous example uses absolute paths stored in the attributes, you can also use relative paths by changing the action code so that it completes the partial path stored in the attribute value; for example, you can use `C:\temp\[% "TYPE" %].png` to open `.png` files that are named according to the `TYPE` attribute values.

Opening a web browser using actions

Another type of useful **Open** action is opening the web browser and accessing certain websites. For example, consider this action:

```
http://www.google.com/search?q=[% "TYPE" %]
```

It will open your default web browser and search for the `TYPE` value using Google, and this action:.

```
https://en.wikipedia.org/w/index.php?search=[% "TYPE" %]
```

will search on Wikipedia.

Getting to know the Python Console

The most direct way to interact with the QGIS **API** (short for **Application Programming Interface**) is through the **Python Console**, which can be opened by going to **Plugins | Python Console**. As you can see in the following screenshot, the **Python Console** is displayed within a new panel below the map:

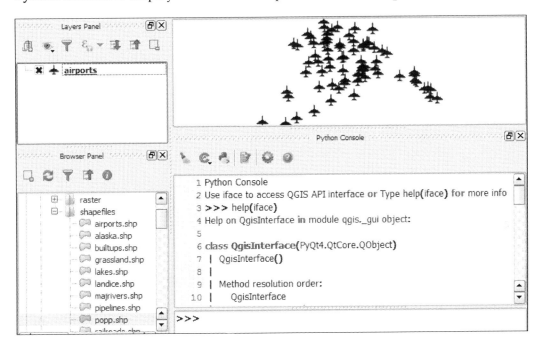

Our access point for interaction with the application, project, and data is the `iface` object. To get a list of all the functions available for `iface`, type `help(iface)`. Alternatively, this information is available online in the **API documentation** at `http://qgis.org/api/classQgisInterface.html`.

Loading and exploring datasets

One of the first things we will want to do is to load some data. For example, to load a vector layer, we use the `addVectorLayer()` function of `iface`:

```
v_layer =
iface.addVectorLayer('C:/Users/anita/Documents/Geodata/qgis_sample_
data/shapefiles/airports.shp','airports','ogr')
```

When we execute this command, `airports.shp` will be loaded using the `ogr` driver and added to the map under the layer name of `airports`. Additionally, this function returns the created `layer` object. Using this `layer` object—which we stored in `v_layer`—we can access vector layer functions, such as `name()`, which returns the layer name and is displayed in the **Layers** list:

```
v_layer.name()
```

This is the output:

```
u'airports'
```

 The u in front of the `airports` layer name shows that the name is returned as a Unicode string.

Of course, the next logical step is to look at the layer's features. The number of features can be accessed using `featureCount()`:

```
v_layer.featureCount()
```

Here is the output:

```
76L
```

This shows us that the airport layer contains 76 features. The `L` in the end shows that it's a numerical value of the long type. In our next step, we will access these features. This is possible using the `getFeatures()` function, which returns a `QgsFeatureIterator` object. With a simple `for` loop, we can then print the `attributes()` of all features in our layer:

```
my_features = v_layer.getFeatures()
for feature in my_features:
    print feature.attributes()
```

This is the output:

```
[1, u'US00157', 78.0, u'Airport/Airfield', u'PA', u'NOATAK' ...
[2, u'US00229', 264.0, u'Airport/Airfield', u'PA', u'AMBLER'...
[3, u'US00186', 585.0, u'Airport/Airfield', u'PABT', u'BETTL...
...
```

 When using the preceding code snippet, it is worth noting that the Python syntax requires proper indentation. This means that, for example, the content of the `for` loop has to be indented, as shown in the preceding code. If Python encounters such errors, it will raise an **Indentation Error**.

You might have noticed that `attributes()` shows us the attribute values, but we don't know the field names yet. To get the field names, we use this code:

```
for field in v_layer.fields():
    print field.name()
```

The output is as follows:

```
ID
fk_region
ELEV
NAME
USE
```

Once we know the field names, we can access specific feature attributes, for example, NAME:

```
for feature in v_layer.getFeatures():

    print feature.attribute('NAME')
```

This is the output:

```
NOATAK
AMBLER
BETTLES
...
```

A quick solution to, for example, sum up the elevation values is as follows:

```
sum([feature.attribute('ELEV') for feature in
v_layer.getFeatures()])
```

Here is the output:

```
22758.0
```

> In the previous example, we took advantage of the fact that Python allows us to create a list by writing a `for` loop inside square brackets. This is called **list comprehension**, and you can read more about it at `https://docs.python.org/2/tutorial/datastructures.html#list-comprehensions`.

Loading raster data is very similar to loading vector data and is done using
`addRasterLayer()`:

```
r_layer = iface.addRasterLayer('C:/Users/anita/Documents/Geodata/qgis_
sample_data/raster/SR_50M_alaska_nad.tif','hillshade')
r_layer.name()
```

The following is the output:

```
u'hillshade'
```

To get the raster layer's size in pixels we can use the `width()` and `height()`
functions, like this:

```
r_layer.width(), r_layer.height()
```

Here is the output:

```
(1754, 1394)
```

If we want to know more about the raster values, we use the layer's data provider
object, which provides access to the raster band statistics. It's worth noting that
we have to use `bandStatistics(1)` instead of `bandStatistics(0)` to access the
statistics of a single-band raster, such as our `hillshade` layer (for example, for the
maximum value):

```
r_layer.dataProvider().bandStatistics(1).maximumValue
```

The output is as follows:

```
251.0
```

Other values that can be accessed like this are `minimumValue`, `range`, `stdDev`, and
`sum`. For a full list, use this line:

```
help(r_layer.dataProvider().bandStatistics(1))
```

Styling layers

Since we now know how to load data, we can continue to style the layers. The
simplest option is to load a premade style (a `.qml` file):

```
v_layer.loadNamedStyle('C:/temp/planes.qml')
v_layer.triggerRepaint()
```

Make sure that you call `triggerRepaint()` to ensure that the map is redrawn to
reflect your changes.

You can create `planes.qml` by saving the airport style you created in *Chapter 2, Viewing Spatial Data* (by going to **Layer Properties** | **Style** | **Save Style** | **QGIS Layer Style File**), or use any other style you like.

Of course, we can also create a style in code. Let's take a look at a basic single symbol renderer. We create a simple symbol with one layer, for example, a yellow diamond:

```
from PyQt4.QtGui import QColor
symbol = QgsMarkerSymbolV2()
symbol.symbolLayer(0).setName('diamond')
symbol.symbolLayer(0).setSize(10)
symbol.symbolLayer(0).setColor(QColor('#ffff00'))
v_layer.rendererV2().setSymbol(symbol)
v_layer.triggerRepaint()
```

A much more advanced approach is to create a **rule-based renderer**. We discussed the basics of rule-based renderers in *Chapter 5, Creating Great Maps*. The following example creates two rules: one for civil-use airports and one for all other airports. Due to the length of this script, I recommend that you use the **Python Console** editor, which you can open by clicking on the **Show editor** button, as shown in the following screenshot:

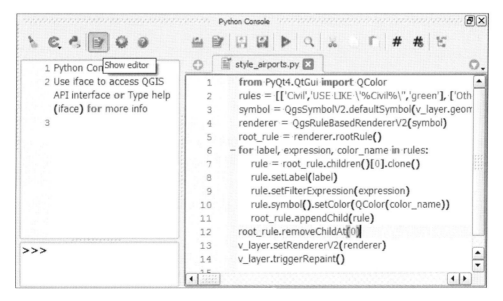

Each rule in this example has a name, a filter expression, and a symbol color. Note how the rules are appended to the renderer's root rule:

```
from PyQt4.QtGui import QColor
rules = [['Civil','USE LIKE \'%Civil%\'','green'], ['Other','USE
NOT LIKE \'%Civil%\'','red']]
symbol = QgsSymbolV2.defaultSymbol(v_layer.geometryType())
renderer = QgsRuleBasedRendererV2(symbol)
root_rule = renderer.rootRule()
for label, expression, color_name in rules:
    rule = root_rule.children()[0].clone()
    rule.setLabel(label)
    rule.setFilterExpression(expression)
    rule.symbol().setColor(QColor(color_name))
    root_rule.appendChild(rule)
root_rule.removeChildAt(0)
v_layer.setRendererV2(renderer)
v_layer.triggerRepaint()
```

To run the script, click on the **Run script** button at the bottom of the editor toolbar.

 If you are interested in reading more about styling vector layers, I recommend Joshua Arnott's post at `http://snorf.net/blog/2014/03/04/symbology-of-vector-layers-in-qgis-python-plugins/`.

Filtering data

To filter vector layer features programmatically, we can specify a subset string. This is the same as defining a **Feature subset** query in in the **Layer Properties | General** section. For example, we can choose to display airports only if their names start with an A:

```
v_layer.setSubsetString("NAME LIKE 'A%'")
```

To remove the filter, just set an empty subset string:

```
v_layer.setSubsetString("")
```

Creating a memory layer

A great way to create a temporary vector layer is by using so-called **memory layers**. Memory layers are a good option for temporary analysis output or visualizations. They are the scripting equivalent of temporary scratch layers, which we used in *Chapter 3, Data Creation and Editing*. Like temporary scratch layers, memory layers exist within a QGIS session and are destroyed when QGIS is closed. In the following example, we create a memory layer and add a polygon feature to it.

Basically, a memory layer is a `QgsVectorLayer` like any other. However, the provider (the third parameter) is not `'ogr'` as in the previous example of loading a file, but `'memory'`. Instead of a file path, the first parameter is a definition string that specifies the geometry type, the CRS, and the attribute table fields (in this case, one integer field called MYNUM and one string field called MYTXT):

```
mem_layer =
QgsVectorLayer("Polygon?crs=epsg:4326&field=MYNUM:integer&field=MYTXT:
string", "temp_layer", "memory")
if not mem_layer.isValid():
    raise Exception("Failed to create memory layer")
```

Once we have created the `QgsVectorLayer` object, we can start adding features to its data provider:

```
mem_layer_provider = mem_layer.dataProvider()
my_polygon = QgsFeature()
my_polygon.setGeometry(
  QgsGeometry.fromRect(QgsRectangle(16,48,17,49)))
my_polygon.setAttributes([10,"hello world"])
mem_layer_provider.addFeatures([my_polygon])
QgsMapLayerRegistry.instance().addMapLayer(mem_layer)
```

 Note how we first create a blank `QgsFeature`, to which we then add geometry and attributes using `setGeometry()` and `setAttributes()`, respectively. When we add the layer to `QgsMapLayerRegistry`, the layer is rendered on the map.

Exporting map images

The simplest option for saving the current map is by using the scripting equivalent of **Save as Image** (under **Project**). This will export the current map to an image file in the same resolution as the map area in the QGIS application window:

```
iface.mapCanvas().saveAsImage('C:/temp/simple_export.png')
```

If we want more control over the size and resolution of the exported image, we need a few more lines of code. The following example shows how we can create our own `QgsMapRendererCustomPainterJob` object and configure to our own liking using custom `QgsMapSettings` for size (`width` and `height`), resolution (`dpi`), map `extent`, and map `layers`:

```
from PyQt4.QtGui import QImage, QPainter
from PyQt4.QtCore import QSize
# configure the output image
width = 800
height = 600
dpi = 92
img = QImage(QSize(width, height), QImage.Format_RGB32)
img.setDotsPerMeterX(dpi / 25.4 * 1000)
img.setDotsPerMeterY(dpi / 25.4 * 1000)
# get the map layers and extent
layers = [ layer.id() for layer in
iface.legendInterface().layers() ]
extent = iface.mapCanvas().extent()
# configure map settings for export
mapSettings = QgsMapSettings()
mapSettings.setMapUnits(0)
mapSettings.setExtent(extent)
mapSettings.setOutputDpi(dpi)
mapSettings.setOutputSize(QSize(width, height))
mapSettings.setLayers(layers)
mapSettings.setFlags(QgsMapSettings.Antialiasing |
QgsMapSettings.UseAdvancedEffects |
QgsMapSettings.ForceVectorOutput | QgsMapSettings.DrawLabeling)
# configure and run painter
p = QPainter()
p.begin(img)
mapRenderer = QgsMapRendererCustomPainterJob(mapSettings, p)
mapRenderer.start()
mapRenderer.waitForFinished()
p.end()
# save the result
img.save("C:/temp/custom_export.png","png")
```

Creating custom geoprocessing scripts using Python

In *Chapter 4, Spatial Analysis*, we used the tools of **Processing Toolbox** to analyze our data, but we are not limited to these tools. We can expand *processing* with our own scripts. The advantages of *processing* scripts over normal Python scripts, such as the ones we saw in the previous section, are as follows:

- Processing automatically generates a graphical user interface for the script to configure the script parameters
- Processing scripts can be used in **Graphical modeler** to create geoprocessing models

As the following screenshot shows, the **Scripts** section is initially empty, except for some **Tools** to add and create new scripts:

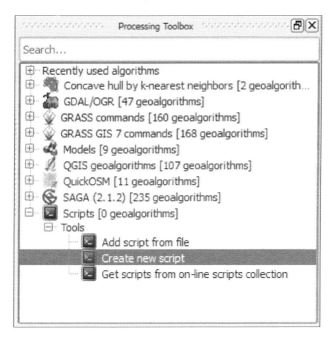

Writing your first Processing script

We will create our first simple script; which fetches some layer information. To get started, double-click on the **Create new script** entry in **Scripts | Tools**. This opens an empty **Script editor** dialog. The following screenshot shows the **Script editor** with a short script that prints the input layer's name on the **Python Console**:

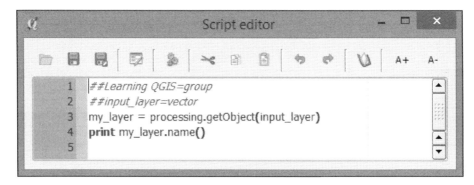

The first line means our script will be put into the Learning QGIS group of scripts, as shown in the following screenshot. The double hashes (##) are Processing syntax and they indicate that the line contains Processing-specific information rather than Python code. The script name is created from the filename you chose when you saved the script. For this example, I have saved the script as my_first_script.py. The second line defines the script input, a vector layer in this case. On the following line, we use Processing's getObject() function to get access to the input layer object, and finally the layer name is printed on the **Python Console**.

You can run the script either directly from within the editor by clicking on the **Run algorithm** button, or by double-clicking on the entry in the **Processing Toolbox**. If you want to change the code, use **Edit script** from the entry context menu, as shown in this screenshot:

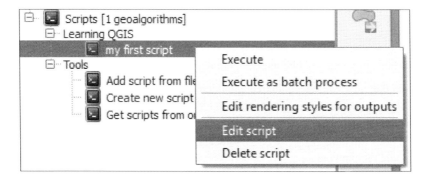

A good way of learning how to write custom scripts for Processing is to take a look at existing scripts, for example, at `https://github.com/qgis/QGIS-Processing/tree/master/scripts`. This is the official script repository, where you can also download scripts using the built-in **Get scripts from on-line scripts collection** tool in the **Processing Toolbox**.

Writing a script with vector layer output

Of course, in most cases, we don't want to just output something on the **Python Console**. That is why the following example shows how to create a vector layer. More specifically, the script creates square polygons around the points in the input layer. The numeric `size` input parameter controls the size of the squares in the `output vector` layer. The default size that will be displayed in the automatically generated dialog is set to `1000000`:

```
##Learning QGIS=group
##input_layer=vector
##size=number 1000000
##squares=output vector
from qgis.core import *
from processing.tools.vector import VectorWriter
# get the input layer and its fields
my_layer = processing.getObject(input_layer)
fields = my_layer.dataProvider().fields()
# create the output vector writer with the same fields
writer = VectorWriter(squares, None, fields, QGis.WKBPolygon,
my_layer.crs())
# create output features
feat = QgsFeature()
for input_feature in my_layer.getFeatures():
    # copy attributes from the input point feature
    attributes = input_feature.attributes()
    feat.setAttributes(attributes)
    # create square polygons
    point = input_feature.geometry().asPoint()
    xmin = point.x() - size/2
    ymin = point.y() - size/2
    square = QgsRectangle(xmin,ymin,xmin+size,ymin+size)
    feat.setGeometry(QgsGeometry.fromRect(square))
    writer.addFeature(feat)
del writer
```

In this script, we use a `VectorWriter` to write the output vector layer. The parameters for creating a `VectorWriter` object are `fileName`, `encoding`, `fields`, `geometryType`, and `crs`.

> The available geometry types are `QGis.WKBPoint`, `QGis.WKBLineString`, `QGis.WKBPolygon`, `QGis.WKBMultiPoint`, `QGis.WKBMultiLineString`, and `QGis.WKBMultiPolygon`. You can also get this list of geometry types by typing `VectorWriter.TYPE_MAP` in the **Python Console**.

Note how we use the fields of the input layer (`my_layer.dataProvider().fields()`) to create the `VectorWriter`. This ensures that the output layer has the same fields (attribute table columns) as the input layer. Similarly, for each feature in the input layer, we copy its attribute values (`input_feature.attributes()`) to the corresponding output feature.

After running the script, the resulting layer will be loaded into QGIS and listed using the output parameter name; in this case, the layer is called `squares`. The following screenshot shows the automatically generated input dialog as well as the output of the script when applied to the airports from our sample dataset:

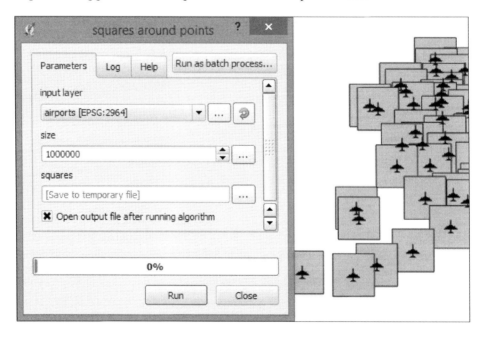

Visualizing the script progress

Especially when executing complex scripts that take a while to finish, it is good practice to display the progress of the script execution in a progress bar. To add a progress bar to the previous script, we can add the following lines of code before and inside the `for` loop that loops through the input features:

```
i = 0
n = my_layer.featureCount()
for input_feature in my_layer.getFeatures():
    progress.setPercentage(int(100*i/n))
    i+=1
```

 Note that we initialize the `i` counter before the loop and increase it inside the loop after updating the progress bar using `progress.setPercentage()`.

Developing your first plugin

When you want to implement interactive tools or very specific graphical user interfaces, it is time to look into plugin development. In the previous exercises, we introduced the QGIS Python API. Therefore, we can now focus on the necessary steps to get our first QGIS plugin started. The great thing about creating plugins for QGIS is that there is a plugin for this! It's called **Plugin Builder**. And while you are at it, also install **Plugin Reloader**, which is very useful for plugin developers. Because it lets you quickly reload your plugin without having to restart QGIS every time you make changes to the code. When you have installed both plugins, your **Plugins** toolbar will look like this:

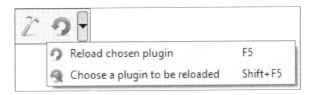

Before we can get started, we also need to install **Qt Designer**, which is the application we will use to design the user interface. If you are using Windows, I recommend **WinPython** (`http://winpython.github.io/`) version 2.7.10.3 (the latest version with Python 2.7 at the time of writing this book), which provides Qt Designer and **Spyder** (an integrated development environment for Python). On Ubuntu, you can install Qt Designer using `sudo apt-get install qt4-designer`. On Mac, you can get the **Qt Creator** installer (which includes Qt Designer) from `http://qt-project.org/downloads`.

Creating the plugin template with Plugin Builder

Plugin Builder will create all the files that we need for our plugin. To create a plugin template, follow these steps:

1. Start **Plugin Builder** and input the basic plugin information, including:
   - **Class name** (one word in camel case; that is, each word starts with an upper case letter)
   - **Plugin name** (a short description)
   - **Module name** (the Python module name for the plugin)

   When you hover your mouse over the input fields in the Plugin Builder dialog, it displays help information, as shown in the following screenshot:

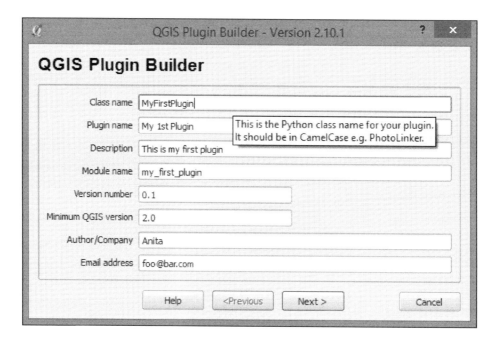

2. Click on **Next** to get to the **About** dialog, where you can enter a more detailed description of what your plugin does. Since we are planning to create the first plugin for learning purposes only, we can just put some random text here and click on **Next**.

3. Now we can select a plugin **Template** and specify a **Text for the menu item** as well as which **Menu** the plugin should be listed in, as shown in the following screenshot. The available templates include **Tool button with dialog**, **Tool button with dock widget**, and **Processing provider**. In this exercise, we'll create a **Tool button with dialog** and click on **Next**:

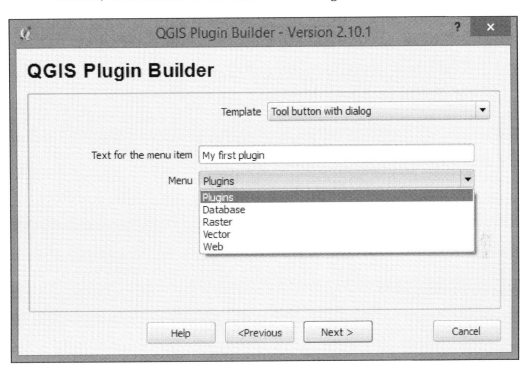

4. The following dialog presents checkboxes, where we can chose which non-essential plugin files should be created. You can select any subset of the provided options and click on **Next**.

5. In the next dialog, we need to specify the plugin **Bug tracker** and the code **Repository**. Again, since we are creating this plugin only for learning purposes, I'm just making up some URLs in the next screenshot, but you should use the appropriate trackers and code repositories if you are planning to make your plugin publicly available:

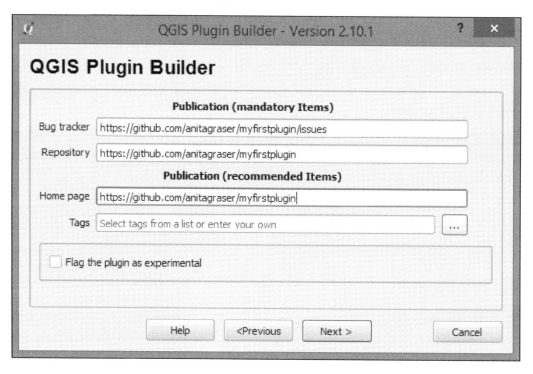

6. Once you click on **Next**, you will be asked to select a folder to store the plugin. You can save it directly in the QGIS plugin folder, `~\.qgis2\python\plugins` on Windows, or `~/.qgis2/python/plugins` on Linux and Mac.

7. Once you have selected the plugin folder, it displays a **Plugin Builder Results** confirmation dialog, which confirms the location of your plugin folder as well as the location of your QGIS plugin folder. As mentioned earlier, I saved directly in the QGIS plugin folder, as you can see in the following screenshot. If you have saved in a different location, you can now move the plugin folder into the QGIS plugins folder to make sure that QGIS can find and load it:

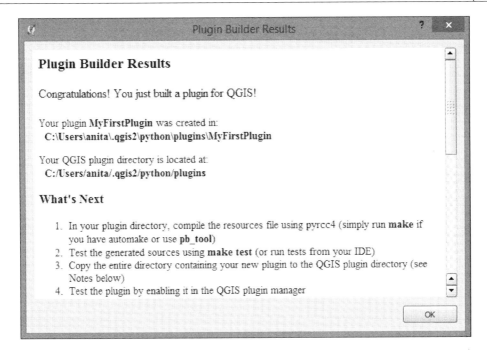

One thing we still have to do is prepare the icon for the plugin toolbar. This requires us to compile the `resources.qrc` file, which **Plugin Builder** created automatically, to turn the icon into usable Python code. This is done on the command line. On Windows, I recommend using the **OSGeo4W shell**, because it makes sure that the environment variables are set in such a way that the necessary tools can be found. Navigate to the plugin folder and run this:

```
pyrcc4 -o resources.py resources.qrc
```

 You can replace the default icon (`icon.png`) to add your own plugin icon. Afterwards, you just have to recompile `resources_rc.qrc` as shown previously.

Restart QGIS and you should now see your plugin listed in the Plugin Manager, as shown here:

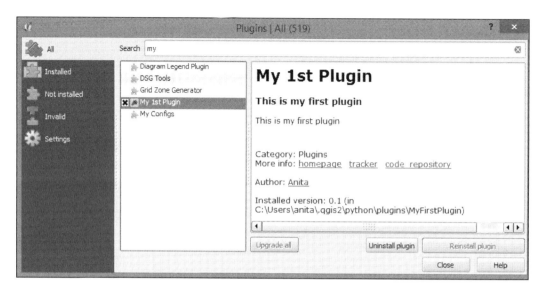

Activate your plugin in the Plugin Manager and you should see it listed in the **Plugins** menu. When you start your plugin, it will display a blank dialog that is just waiting for you to customize it.

Customizing the plugin GUI

To customize the blank default plugin dialog, we use **Qt Designer**. You can find the dialog file in the plugin folder. In my case, it is called my_first_plugin_dialog_base.ui (derived from the module name I specified in Plugin Builder). When you open your plugin's .ui file in Qt Designer, you will see the blank dialog. Now you can start adding widgets by dragging and dropping them from the **Widget Box** on the left-hand side of the Qt Designer window. In the following screenshot, you can see that I added a **Label** and a drop-down list widget (listed as **Combo Box** in the **Widgetbox**). You can change the label text to Layer by double-clicking on the default label text. Additionally, it is good practice to assign descriptive names to the widget objects; for example, I renamed the combobox to layerCombo, as you can see here in the bottom-right corner:

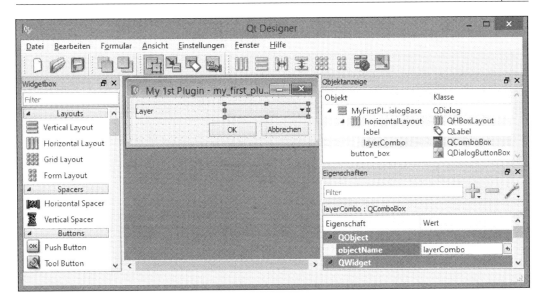

Once you are finished with the changes to the plugin dialog, you can save them. Then you can go back to QGIS. In QGIS, you can now configure **Plugin Reloader** by clicking on the **Choose a plugin to be reloaded** button in the **Plugins** toolbar and selecting your plugin. If you now click on the **Reload Plugin** button and the press your plugin button, your new plugin dialog will be displayed.

Implementing plugin functionality

As you have certainly noticed, the layer combobox is still empty. To populate the combobox with a list of loaded layers, we need to add a few lines of code to my_first_plugin.py (located in the plugin folder). More specifically, we expand the run() method:

```
def run(self):
    """Run method that performs all the real work"""
    # show the dialog
    self.dlg.show()
    # clear the combo box to list only current layers
    self.dlg.layerCombo.clear()
    # get the layers and add them to the combo box
    layers = QgsMapLayerRegistry.instance().mapLayers().values()
    for layer in layers:
        if layer.type() == QgsMapLayer.VectorLayer:
            self.dlg.layerCombo.addItem( layer.name(), layer )
    # Run the dialog event loop
    result = self.dlg.exec_()
```

```
    # See if OK was pressed
    if result:
        # Check which layer was selected
        index = self.dlg.layerCombo.currentIndex()
        layer = self.dlg.layerCombo.itemData(index)
        # Display information about the layer
        QMessageBox.information(self.iface.mainWindow(),"Learning
QGIS","%s has %d features." %(layer.name(),layer.featureCount()))
```

You also have to add the following import line at the top of the script to avoid NameErrors concerning QgsMapLayerRegistry and QMessageBox:

```
    from qgis.core import *
    from PyQt4.QtGui import QMessageBox
```

Once you are done with the changes to my_first_plugin.py, you can save the file and use the **Reload Plugin** button in QGIS to reload your plugin. If you start your plugin now, the combobox will be populated with a list of all layers in the current QGIS project, and when you click on **OK**, you will see a message box displaying the number of features in the selected layer.

Creating a custom map tool

While the previous exercise showed how to create a custom GUI that enables the user to interact with QGIS, in this exercise, we will go one step further and implement our own custom **map tool** similar to the default **Identify tool**. This means that the user can click on the map and the tool reports which feature on the map was clicked on.

To this end, we create another **Tool button with dialog** plugin template called MyFirstMapTool. For this tool, we do not need to create a dialog. Instead, we have to write a bit more code than we did in the previous example. First, we create our custom map tool class, which we call IdentifyFeatureTool. Besides the __init__() constructor, this tool has a function called canvasReleaseEvent() that defines the actions of the tool when the mouse button is released (that is, when you let go of the mouse button after pressing it):

```
    class IdentifyFeatureTool(QgsMapToolIdentify):
        def __init__(self, canvas):
            QgsMapToolIdentify.__init__(self, canvas)
        def canvasReleaseEvent(self, mouseEvent):
            print "canvasReleaseEvent"
            # get features at the current mouse position
            results = self.identify(mouseEvent.x(),mouseEvent.y(),
                        self.TopDownStopAtFirst, self.VectorLayer)
```

```
        if len(results) > 0:
            # signal that a feature was identified
            self.emit( SIGNAL( "geomIdentified" ),
                       results[0].mLayer, results[0].mFeature)
```

You can paste the preceding code at the end of the `my_first_map_tool.py` code.
Of course, we now have to put our new map tool to good use. In the `initGui()`
function, we replace the `run()` method with a new `map_tool_init()` function.
Additionally, we define that our map tool is checkable; this means that the user can
click on the tool icon to activate it and click on it again to deactivate it:

```
def initGui(self):
    # create the toolbar icon and menu entry
    icon_path = ':/plugins/MyFirstMapTool/icon.png'
    self.map_tool_action=self.add_action(
        icon_path,
        text=self.tr(u'My 1st Map Tool'),
        callback=self.map_tool_init,
        parent=self.iface.mainWindow())
    self.map_tool_action.setCheckable(True)
```

The new `map_tool_init()` function takes care of activating or deactivating our
map tool when the button is clicked on. During activation, it creates an instance of
our custom `IdentifyFeatureTool`, and the following line connects the map tool's
`geomIdentified` signal to the `do_something()` function, which we will discuss in a
moment. Similarly, when the map tool is deactivated, we disconnect the signal and
restore the previous map tool:

```
def map_tool_init(self):
    # this function is called when the map tool icon is clicked
    print "maptoolinit"
    canvas = self.iface.mapCanvas()
    if self.map_tool_action.isChecked():
        # when the user activates the tool
        self.prev_tool = canvas.mapTool()
        self.map_tool_action.setChecked( True )
        self.map_tool = IdentifyFeatureTool(canvas)
        QObject.connect(self.map_tool,SIGNAL("geomIdentified"),
                        self.do_something )
        canvas.setMapTool(self.map_tool)
        QObject.connect(canvas,SIGNAL("mapToolSet(QgsMapTool *)"),
                        self.map_tool_changed)
    else:
        # when the user deactivates the tool
```

```
QObject.disconnect(canvas,SIGNAL("mapToolSet(QgsMapTool *)"
                                 ),self.map_tool_changed)
canvas.unsetMapTool(self.map_tool)
print "restore prev tool %s" %(self.prev_tool)
canvas.setMapTool(self.prev_tool)
```

Our new custom `do_something()` function is called when our map tool is used to successfully identify a feature. For this example, we simply print the feature's attributes on the **Python Console**. Of course, you can get creative here and add your desired custom functionality:

```
def do_something(self, layer, feature):
    print feature.attributes()
```

Finally, we also have to handle the case when the user switches to a different map tool. This is similar to the case of the user deactivating our tool in the `map_tool_init()` function:

```
def map_tool_changed(self):
    print "maptoolchanged"
    canvas = self.iface.mapCanvas()
    QObject.disconnect(canvas,SIGNAL("mapToolSet(QgsMapTool *)"),
                       self.map_tool_changed)
    canvas.unsetMapTool(self.map_tool)
    self.map_tool_action.setChecked(False)
```

You also have to add the following import line at the top of the script to avoid errors concerning `QObject`, `QgsMapTool`, and others:

```
from qgis.core import *
from qgis.gui import *
from PyQt4.QtCore import *
```

When you are ready, you can reload the plugin and try it. You should have the **Python Console** open to be able to follow the plugin's outputs. The first thing you will see when you activate the plugin in the toolbar is that it prints `maptoolinit` on the console. Then, if you click on the map, it will print `canvasReleaseEvent`, and if you click on a feature, it will also display the feature's attributes. Finally, if you change to another map tool (for example, the **Pan Map** tool) it will print `maptoolchanged` on the console and the icon in the plugin toolbar will be unchecked.

Summary

In this chapter, we covered the different ways to extend QGIS using actions and Python scripting. We started with different types of actions and then continued to the **Python Console**, which offers a direct, interactive way to interact with the QGIS Python API. We also used the editor that is part of the **Python Console** panel and provides a better way to work on longer scripts containing loops or even multiple class and function definitions. Next, we applied our knowledge of PyQGIS to develop custom tools for the **Processing Toolbox**. These tools profit from Processing's automatic GUI generation capabilities, and they can be used in **Graphical modeler** to create geopreocessing models. Last but not least, we developed a basic plugin based on a **Plugin Builder** template.

With this background knowledge, you can now start your own PyQGIS experiments. There are several web and print resources that you can use to learn more about QGIS Python scripting. For the updated QGIS API documentation, check out `http://qgis.org/api/`. If you are interested in more PyQGIS recipes, take a look at *PyQGIS Developer Cookbook* at `http://docs.qgis.org/testing/en/docs/pyqgis_developer_cookbook` and QGIS programming books offered by *Packt Publishing*, as well as Gary Sherman's book *The PyQGIS Programmer's Guide, Locate Press*.

Index

Symbols

2.5D style
  creating 129
3D web map
  exporting 154, 155
.ui file
  reference link 64
  used, for creating feature form 64

A

absolute paths 48
actions
  used, for adding functionality 157, 158
  used, for opening files 160
  used, for opening web browser 160
advanced vector styling
  2.5D style, creating 129
  about 117
  categorized styles, using for
      nominal data 123
  color ramps, creating 121, 122
  color ramps, using 121, 122
  data-defined symbology, creating 126, 127
  dynamic heatmap style, creating 128
  graduated style, creating 118-120
  live layer effects, adding 130, 131
  multiple styles, working with 131, 132
  rule-based style, creating for
      road layers 124, 125
airport style
  example 36-39
Android 1
ArcCatalog 10
ArcPy 157

Atlas feature
  used, for creating map series 150
attribute form 62
attributes
  editing 60
  editing, in attribute table 60-62
  new values, calculating 65, 66
attribute table
  attributes, editing 60-62
  join results, checking 70
  used, with print maps 149
autogenerate
  reference 63
  used, for creating feature form 63
automated geoprocessing
  with graphical modeler 108-111

B

background maps
  loading 45-47
basic map
  creating 141
  legend, adding 144
  north arrow image, adding 144
  scalebar, adding 143
batch-processing 107, 108

C

categorized styles
  using, for nominal data 123
color models 127
color names 127
color ramps
  creating 121, 122
  using 121, 122

ISO basic Latin alphabet
  reference link 3

K

kernel functions
  reference link 92

L

label placement
  line labels, configuring 137
  point labels, configuring 137
  polygon labels, configuring 137, 138
labels
  activating 133, 134
  background, configuring 136
  buffers, configuring 136
  formatting 135, 136
  placement, controlling 136
  placing, manually 138, 139
  rendering 139, 140
  shadows, configuring 136
  text styles, customizing 135
landmass style
  example 42-45
Layer Properties
  join, setting up 69
Leaflet
  about 151
  URL 154
linear option 26
lines
  converting 96-98
line styles
  creating 39-42
Linux 1
list comprehension
  about 163
  reference link 163
live layer effects
  adding 130, 131

M

Mac OS X 1
map tiles
  creating 153, 154

measuring tools
  using 60
memory layers 167
Memory Layer Saver plugin 71
models
  documenting 112, 113
  sharing 112, 113
mouse
  used, for selecting features 54
MSSQL 27
multiline labels
  enabling 135
multiple datasets
  batch-processing 107, 108

N

nearest neighbors
  obtaining 95, 96
network drive 48
Notepad++ 48

O

OfflineEditing plugin 13
OGC web services
  data, loading from 29-31
  reference link 29
OGR SQL
  URL 28
on the fly reprojection 22
Open Geospatial Consortium (OGC) 17
OpenLayers 3 151
Oracle Spatial 27
OSGeo4W
  about 2
  URL 2
OSGeo4W installer 2
OSGeo4W shell 177
overview map
  creating 148

P

plugin
  developing 173
  implementing 179, 180

QGIS, releases
  developer version
      (DEV, master, or testing) 2
  latest release (LR) 2
  long-term release (LTR) 1
  reference link 2
Qt Creator installer
  URL 173
Qt Designer 173, 178

R

raster and vector data
  combining 86
  converting between 86, 87
  heatmap, creating from points 92, 93
  raster layer statistics, accessing 87-90
  vector layer statistics, accessing 87-90
  zonal statistics, computing 90-92
raster data
  analyzing 79
  converting 67, 68
  elevation/terrain data, analyzing 82-84
  raster calculator, using 84-86
  rasters, clipping 79-81
  reprojecting 67, 68
raster files
  loading 23, 24
Rasterize tool 87
raster layers
  styling 32-35
raster maps
  georeferencing 24-26
relative path 48
resampling method 26
river styles
  example 39-42
road styles
  example 39-42
rule-based style
  creating, for road layers 124, 125

S

script
  progress, visualizing of 173
  writing, with vector layer output 171, 172

second-order polynomial transformation 26
selection tools 53
self-intersecting polygons error 74
shapefiles 18
Shuttle Radar Topography Mission (SRTM)
  URL 81
sliver polygons 75
snapping
  used, for topologically correct editing 59
spatial databases
  about 113
  data, adding 76, 77
SpatiaLite
  about 27
  data, aggregating 115, 116
  location, selecting 113-115
  reference link 114
  URL 113
spatial queries
  used, for selecting features 55, 56
Spyder 173
SQLite
  about 27
  URL 27
standalone installer 2
System for Automated Geoscientific
      Analyses (SAGA) GIS 2

T

tabular data
  joining 68, 69
  join results, checking in attribute table 70
  join, setting up in Layer Properties 69
temporary scratch layers
  using 70, 71
terrain analysis tools 81
thin-plate spline algorithm 26
third-order polynomial transformation 26
topological errors
  checking for 71
  finding, Topology Checker
      plugin used 72-74
  fixing 71
  invalid geometry errors, fixing 74, 75

U

Ubuntu
  QGIS, installing on 8-10
Unix 1

V

v.sample GRASS tool 101
vector and raster analysis
  performing, with Processing plugin 94, 95
vector data
  converting 67, 68
  loading, from files 18-20
  reprojecting 67, 68
vector geometries
  advanced digitizing tools, using 58, 59
  basic digitizing tools, using 57
  editing 57
  snapping, using 59
vector layer output
  script, writing with 171, 172
vector layers
  creating 51-53
  reference link 166
  styling 35, 36

W

web browser
  opening, actions used 160
Web Coverage Services (WCS) 29
Web Feature Services (WFS) 29, 31
web maps
  3D web map, exporting 154, 155
  about 151
  exporting 151, 152
  map tiles, creating 153, 154
Web Map Services (WMS) 29
Windows
  about 1
  QGIS, installing on 2-7
WinPython
  URL 173
WKT
  about 21
  reference link 21

Z

zonal statistics
  computing 90-92

Thank you for buying
Learning QGIS
Third Edition

About Packt Publishing

Packt, pronounced 'packed', published its first book, *Mastering phpMyAdmin for Effective MySQL Management*, in April 2004, and subsequently continued to specialize in publishing highly focused books on specific technologies and solutions.

Our books and publications share the experiences of your fellow IT professionals in adapting and customizing today's systems, applications, and frameworks. Our solution-based books give you the knowledge and power to customize the software and technologies you're using to get the job done. Packt books are more specific and less general than the IT books you have seen in the past. Our unique business model allows us to bring you more focused information, giving you more of what you need to know, and less of what you don't.

Packt is a modern yet unique publishing company that focuses on producing quality, cutting-edge books for communities of developers, administrators, and newbies alike. For more information, please visit our website at www.packtpub.com.

About Packt Open Source

In 2010, Packt launched two new brands, Packt Open Source and Packt Enterprise, in order to continue its focus on specialization. This book is part of the Packt Open Source brand, home to books published on software built around open source licenses, and offering information to anybody from advanced developers to budding web designers. The Open Source brand also runs Packt's Open Source Royalty Scheme, by which Packt gives a royalty to each open source project about whose software a book is sold.

Writing for Packt

We welcome all inquiries from people who are interested in authoring. Book proposals should be sent to author@packtpub.com. If your book idea is still at an early stage and you would like to discuss it first before writing a formal book proposal, then please contact us; one of our commissioning editors will get in touch with you.

We're not just looking for published authors; if you have strong technical skills but no writing experience, our experienced editors can help you develop a writing career, or simply get some additional reward for your expertise.

open source
community experience distilled

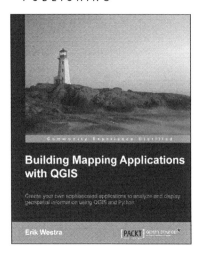

**Building Mapping Applications
with QGIS**

**Building Mapping Applications
with QGIS**

Create your own sophisticated applications to analyze and display geospatial information using QGIS and Python

Erik Westra

Building Mapping Applications with QGIS

ISBN: 978-1-78398-466-4   Paperback: 264 pages

Create your own sophisticated applications to analyze and display geospatial information using QGIS and Python

1. Make use of the geospatial capabilities of QGIS within your Python programs.

2. Build complete standalone mapping applications based on QGIS and Python.

3. Use QGIS as a Python geospatial development environment.

**QGIS Python Programming
Cookbook**

Over 140 recipes to help you turn QGIS from a desktop GIS tool into a powerful automated geospatial framework

Joel Lawhead

QGIS Python Programming Cookbook

ISBN: 978-1-78398-498-5   Paperback: 340 pages

Over 140 recipes to help you turn QGIS from a desktop GIS tool into a powerful automated geospatial framework

1. Use Python and QGIS to create and transform data, produce appealing GIS visualizations, and build complex map layouts.

2. Learn undocumented features of the new QGIS processing module.

3. A set of user-friendly recipes that can automate the entire geospatial workflows by connecting Python GIS building blocks into comprehensive processes.

Please check **www.PacktPub.com** for information on our titles

Printed in Great Britain
by Amazon